KU-714-734

Witches, Sirens and Soothsayers

ORRA
Iam
bli
cus
libri iii
OPUS
XII
paracel-
sus

Witches, Sirens and Soothsayers

SUSANNAH MARRIOTT

For the Falmouth moonwalkers, especially Charlotte.

previous page: ***Love Potion*****, Evelyn de Morgan, 1903, British**

Her painting depicts a witch—clearly identified by her red hair, yellow gown and the black cat at her feet—mixing a potion for the couple embracing outside her window.

Introduction

"Hie thee thither, That I may pour my spirits in thine ear..."

LADY MACBETH IN *MACBETH*, WILLIAM SHAKESPEARE

Witches hold a spell over popular culture centuries after the witch obsession of the "burning times" sent so many innocent women to their deaths. Though she is an object of fear, loathing and denigration, the witch remains as attractive, as titillating and as alluring as she is repulsive. Writers and artists, historians, cultural commentators and spiritual seekers keep the iconic Hag, the Wise Woman and the Goddess alive in our shared imagination, our intellect and in our hearts.

Storytellers, writers and illustrators draw inspiration from the appearance of hags and crones in folk tales. By telling their stories afresh, and embroidering them with motifs that have resonance for modern audiences, writers and artists ensure that witches continue to terrify and thrill. Think of the self-parodying Disney movie *Enchanted*, which in 2007 played on stereotypes of the witch—her poisoned apple, magic mirror, erotic lure and shape-shifting powers—to drive the story of a fairytale princess's quest for love in contemporary New York City.

right: **The Kobal Collection, Disney Enterprises, Barry Wetcher 2007, American**

Susan Sarandon plays the gloriously stereotyped Queen Narissa in the 2007 movie *Enchanted*, channeling Disney's back catalogue of witch-like figures, from Snow White's wicked stepmother to Cruella De Vil.

Historians and cultural theorists find the witch trials of the early modern era so potent a topic of scholarly study that university shelves groan with learned, vibrant works on the subject. Despite scholarly apologies as far back as the 1970s for returning to topics such as the history of witchcraft in Salem, that many considered overworked even then, the lives and deaths of so-called witches and their accusers are poured over afresh with each new intake of undergraduates on courses not only in history, but in literature and women's studies.

Witchcraft or the worship of the Goddess has woven a spell over so many seekers on the spiritual path that paganism is the fastest growing form of religion in the West, with young women finding particular appeal in its diverse forms, its ability to adapt the individual and its focus on communion with the earth.

So why all this continuing attention on the witch? One answer might be that the witch allows us to take a look at stuff we usually sweep under the carpet. Dangerous stuff. She inhabits extreme situations and exhibits troubling emotions that we might prefer to avoid in everyday life—even in the 21st century. The witch of fairytale lore, in literature and in history is tied up with death and evil, fear and violence, sexuality and power, ugliness and justice, and because she stands apart from regular society, her very existence can be a form of protest against it. As an example, we might look at the teenage girls in Salem who exhibited forms of "possession". One of them, 16-year-old Elizabeth Knapp, seems to "try on" being a handmaid of the devil as a way of expressing her discontent at her lot—at being a lowly servant in a prosperous home, with no route to education or access to life's pretty things. Toying with demonic possession allows her—a teenage girl and so the lowest of the low in her society—to openly curse her employer and the minister of the town, to blaspheme and talk dirty, to contemplate suicide and murder and above all, to be taken seriously by those who do hold power. How cool is that? And once she's gained some attention, she can throw off the mantle of witchcraft by repudiating the devil and choosing to live a respectable life.

To mothers, the witch offers a way of thinking about the inevitable conflicts of motherhood—of examining the fear that comes with intense love, and the rebellion that many of us feel when tied down to domesticity with small children. This bad mother enacts our darkest fantasies so we don't have to and gives words to our unsayable anxieties.

The witch's sexual allure—which challenges conventional norms of feminine beauty and age—continues to be an inspiration, too. The witch in cultures the world over is assertive and sexually confident into old age—and needs no man to confirm it. More than this, she has the ability to step outside the norms society imposes on the female body by slipping between forms: one moment she is a crooked old woman, the next a bounding hare, jumping with sexual energy, a comely wench or a sage old bird, taking flight as an all-seeing wise owl. The witch is ever able to transform herself and the forces of nature, breaking the chains thrown around her both by social mores and the laws of physics.

Witches empower modern women to take risks: to think and act like her is to feel strong. Powerful enough to walk moor and mountain alone by night, to reclaim city streets and protest against militarism. To become the witches they can never silence, who have learned what it is to be free.

This book is a pick-and-mix celebration of the enduring traits that endear the witch to us, and her many, often contradictory, forms. Here we encounter her as diviner, fortune-teller and shaman, as charmer and

BYAM SHAW
THERE WAS·AN
OLD WOMAN WHO
RODE·ON·A·BROOM
With a high gee ho
gee humble

blesser, juggler and high-wire walker, as charlatan and madam, bad mother and anti-housewife, as green doctor and wise woman, dominatrix and nature goddess, prophetess and muse. Her many identities are refracted in the mirrors of poetry and prose, fable and proverb, and in illustration and fine art. These reflections are juxtaposed with mini essays that explore aspects of the witch's varied histories across the globe and through the centuries. Along the way we will meet contemporary writers, film-makers and political animals who have engaged fruitfully with myths of witchcraft, and we will learn from those who explore goddess-centric faith traditions. They include a Romany fortune-teller and New York's number one contemporary witch, one of the leading Shakespearean actresses of our day, an Anglican priest who writes about and rails against the dark arts, and historians who have fought to clear the names of those falsely accused of witchcraft in Salem.

In the end, the witch in this book is much more than a figure of persecution and misunderstanding; she is someone whose life we might like to sample for a while. For what wife is not tempted by the idea of leaving her husband in bed and shooting into the sky on a broomstick to carouse with a bunch of girlfriends? Who has never marvelled at the magic of Mother Earth? Wouldn't we all, if we could, be the enchantress Circe, who turns the dull men in a room into pigs and spellbinds Mr Big? Tune in to the elements, look into the future and transform into a myriad forms at the wrinkle of a nose? Who wouldn't be a witch?

Susannah Marriott, Cornwall 2008

left: **Old Woman on Broom, Byam Shaw, 1901, British**

High on her own power, this liberated old woman sets out to visit the man in the moon, willingly abandoning her home and all the chores it entails.

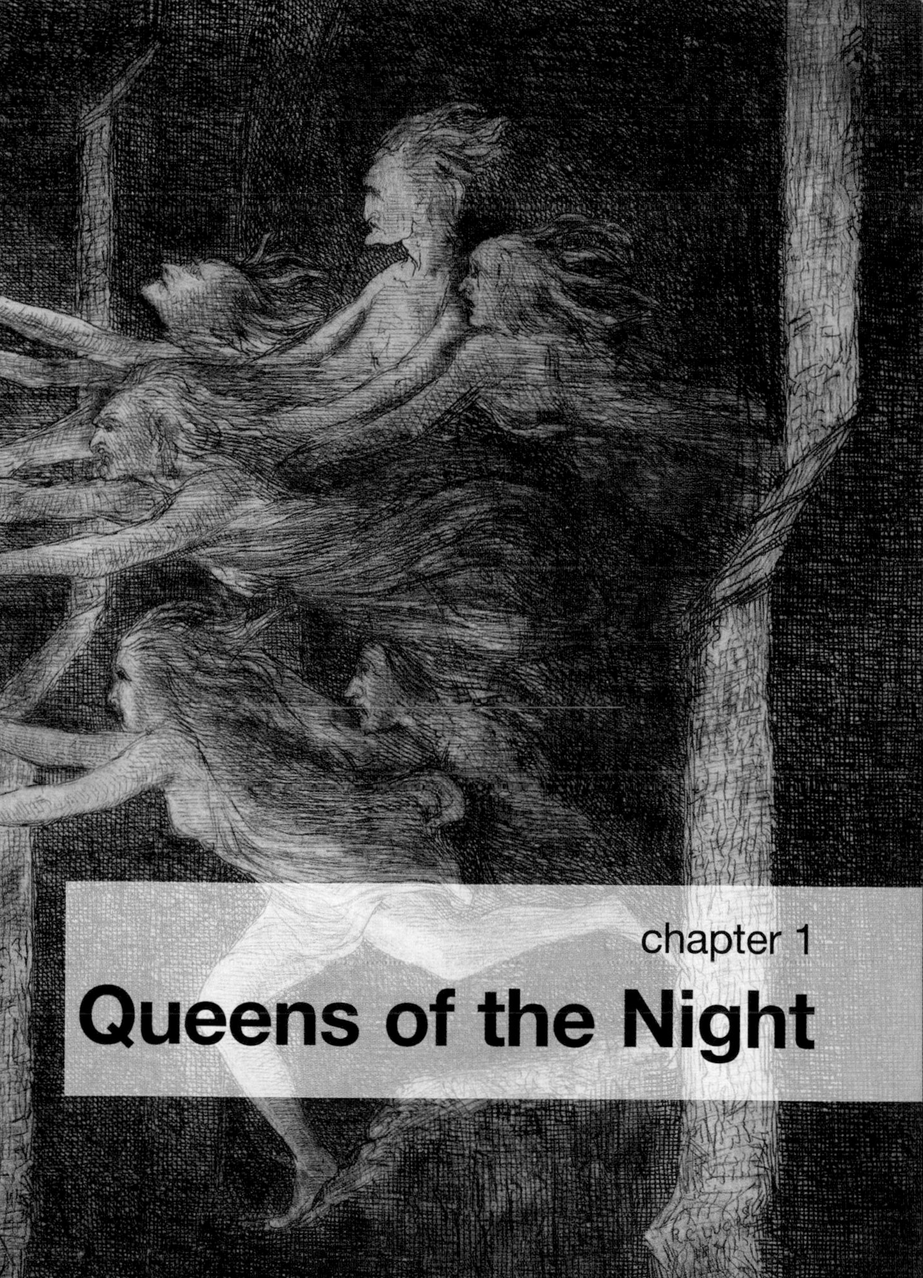

chapter 1

Queens of the Night

Dark as night

In the topsy-turvy world of witchcraft, where night is day and day is night, "fair is foul, and foul is fair", those without powers by day, such as poor old ladies—become gifted after sundown. Across cultures, witches are regarded as supernaturally endowed queens of the night skies, and this is expressed in the titles they are given, such as *donni di notti*, "night women", in Sicily. Light is universally associated with goodness, and so absence of light and the Sun with its opposite, branding creatures who roam beneath the Moon as evil. The darkness of those few nights each month when the Moon takes its brief absence might be likened to a death, and as a creature of the night, the witch is thought to have an entry pass to this realm, too.

During the darkness of night, it becomes difficult to perceive using sight, the sense we most rely on by day, which heightens anxiety about the unknown and exaggerates irrational fears. Darkness is associated also with the power of that other hidden realm, the unconscious, which governs dreaming and uncontrollable instinctive reactions that betray our deepest desires and fears. The witch has extra-sensory perception, or second sight, and so is able not only to see by night, but to infiltrate our secret inner realm, shading our hopes and mining our dark nights of the soul.

Superstition suggests that ordinary folk who venture outdoors by moonlight risk bad dreams, ill fortune or madness. Children might be taught to draw the curtains to avoid seeing the Moon through glass (a portent of destruction) and when outdoors not to draw attention to the Moon, the witch's planet, by pointing. Nor should they try to count the numberless stars in the firmament; that way lies the wrath of the

Man in the Moon and perhaps lunacy. Those who do catch a chance reflection are urged to repeat a protective incantation, such as "I see the Moon and the Moon sees me; God bless the Moon and God bless me."

In Taoism, the Full Moon in the night sky stands for the eye of spiritual knowledge amid the darkness. The witch uses her affinity with the Moon to claim knowledge of past, present and future, and advocates Moon divination magic. The first sighting of the New Moon is considered a time of new-beginning magic that one can court by bowing, curtseying or saluting three times. If you turn over the silver in your pocket (or turn your apron) at the same time, Lady Luck will be yours before that Moon is out. The Moon is especially ripe for love divination. It waxes, or grows full, suffusing the Earth with light, then wanes, growing small and dark, just as the female body swells to bring forth new life. Night-time is therefore also associated with sexuality and fecundity. By reciting words of power while gazing at the Moon or climbing closer to it, or refracting its image through a silk handkerchief, a girl might share in the witch's magical powers and discern the man of her dreams.

previous page: ***Horseman Fleeing from Witches*, Richard Cockle Lucas, 19th century, British**

A horseman fleeing a gaggle of naked witches displays the typical fear with which mankind approaches the subject of witches. The witches are borne on the air and seem in control of the foul weather.

"Deep night, dark night,
the silent of the night,
The time of night when Troy
was set on fire;
The time when screech-owls
cry and bandogs howl,
And spirits walk and ghosts
break up their graves."

***HENRY VI*, WILLIAM SHAKESPEARE**

left: ***The Evil Queen in Disguise*, Charles B. Falls, 1913, British**

The witch appears as a restless wanderer who roams the land by night when most folks stay safe at home.

previous page: ***Mad Women in the Street*, Artist unknown, 17th century, French**

Women are drawn out to dance by the light of the moon. They need no other illumination, unlike the men spying on their midnight merrymaking. The 16th-century Swiss philosopher and theologian Erasmus tells us it was widely believed in antiquity that witches could draw the Moon and stars down to Earth with their spells.

The Woman in the Moon

Witches, claims the Elizabethan writer Reginald Scot, have the power to "pull downe the moone and the stars". The Moon is the planet most often linked with women. In its ever-mutating shape and size (every night of the month it looks slightly different), and the length of time it takes to move through a complete cycle, it echoes a woman's average 28-day menstrual cycle, and, some say, her fickle moods and emotions. In some cultures, it was thought that the Moon caused a woman to menstruate, her menses referred to as her "moon" and different parts of the cycle were compared to the Moon as it waxes (swells) and wanes (grows small), peaking at ovulation and menstruation. If our bodies have something of the spheres abut them and correspond to extra-terrestrial rhythms, surely we must be privy to supernatural powers from which men are excluded: we are all potential witches.

The Moon's inconstancy links it with notions of birth, death and rebirth, but also with peril. What if the Moon didn't return after dying each month? The Greek historian Plutarch tells a tale about the Moon, who asks her mother to make her a petticoat "fit and proportionate" for her body. Why, how is it possible (replied her mother) to knit or weave a petticoat to fit well about her form considering "I see thee one while full, another while croissant or in the wane and pointed with tips of horns, and sometime again half round." This sounds dangerous; the daughter is outside everyone's control, even her maker's, and the mention of horns suggests an infernal root of such inconstancy.

The French philosopher-scientist Bernard le Bovier de Fontenelle claimed that with a telescope one could see not the Man in the Moon, but a woman, with characteristics remarkably akin to those of the stereotypical witch: "She had a pretty good face, but her cheeks are now sunken, her nose is lengthened, her forehead and chin are now prominent to such an extent, that all her charms have vanished, and I fear for her days." The poets Penelope Shuttle and Peter Redgrove goes further, finding the Moon in the woman. They suggest that with the aid of a speculum and mirror, every woman can detect her own inner Moon: the globe-like cervix resting in a crescent of tissue at the mouth of the womb, which changes in appearance day by day and night by night through the course of the menstrual cycle.

following page: **Detail from *Queen of the Night*, Henri Fantin-Latour, *c.*1900, French**

The Woman in the Moon gazes languidly down to an Earth lit by lunar light as the Moon creeps from behind a veil of clouds.

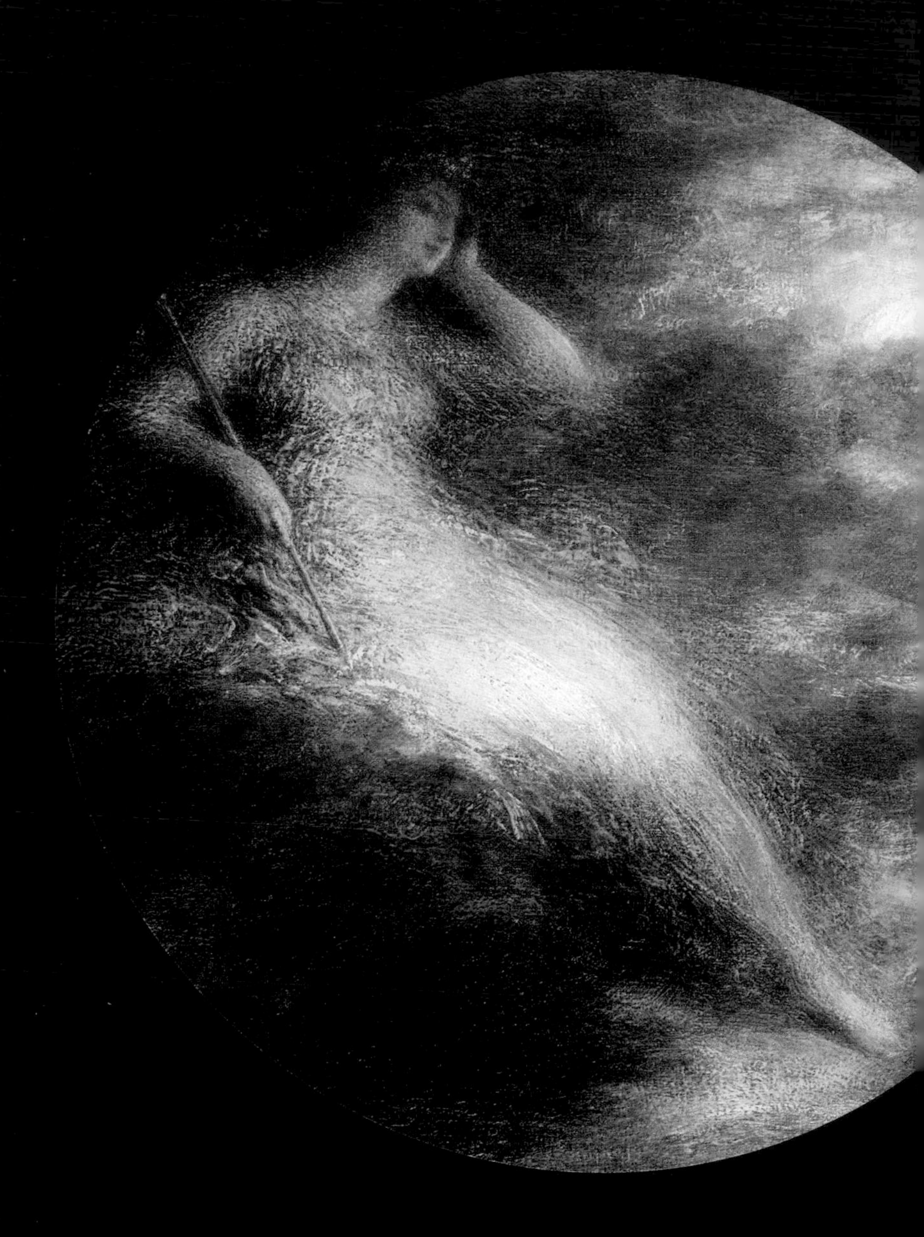

"There is something haunting in the light of the moon; it has all the dispassionateness of a disembodied soul, and something of its inconceivable mystery."

***LORD JIM*, JOSEPH CONRAD**

Moon goddesses

Over the centuries, a number of female deities have been linked with the Moon, from the chaste to the fearsome. They are often pictured in triple form, reflecting three phases of the Moon. The New Moon is a chaste maiden full of promise; the Full Moon a mother goddess ripe with new life; and the Dark Moon is represented by the Hag, or Queen of the Underworld. In this triumverate, the New Moon is the fierce, virginal huntress of the Greek pantheon, Artemis, and her Roman alter-ego Diana (see page 28). The Dark Moon belongs to the witch Hecate, and the Full Moon to the sensual, rounded Selene, who rides across the night sky on horseback or in a chariot drawn by winged white steeds. One of the older generation of Greek gods, Selene bears the children of gods and seduces mortal men, and she is so enchanted by her young mortal lover Endymion that she causes him to slumber "moon-struck" in a charmed sleep to preserve his youth forever. Aside from sleeping beauty, she can induce raging lunacy (in her Roman incarnation she is Luna).

Hecate combines many of the attributes of other lunar goddesses. Her powers extend over Earth, sea and heavens, but it is with the underworld that she is most often associated, patroness of all things dark, deathly and uncanny. This mistress of the shades also is depicted in a three-form aspect, as three figures facing in different directions or with three heads—snake, dog and horse—or presiding over the point where three roads meet. At her side are her familiars, a black bitch and a cat. Though Hecate is considered the dark goddess, she plays a role in regeneration. It is she who with flaming torches guides the Earth goddess Demeter through the dark of night to find her daughter Persephone, without whom spring would not return each year. Without death, there can be no new life, this witch teaches us. Guardians of the darkness and of death in many cultures also guard those near life, and coax them through the gates of the birth canal. Hulda, the night-riding sky goddess of the pre-Christian Germanic tradition, is goddess of death and birth, like Hel, the Norse queen of the underworld, who governs a moonlit place of cold and mists, but also presides over birth and reincarnation, rewarding those who do good deeds with new life, and condemning the bad or ill-mannered to a life of punishment.

"[Zeus] gave [Hecate] splendid gifts, to have a share of the earth and the unfruitful sea. She received honour also in starry heaven, and is honoured exceedingly by the deathless gods. For to this day, whenever any one of men on earth offers rich sacrifices and prays for favour according to custom, he calls upon Hecate. Great honour comes full easily to him whose prayers the goddess receives favourably, and she bestows wealth upon him; for the power surely is with her."

***THE THEOGONY OF HESIOD* (*c.*8TH CENTURY BCE)**
TRANS. HUGH G. EVELYN-WHITE

following page: ***Hecate*, Johfra Boffchart, 1973, Dutch**

In *Hecate* the goddess of sorcery sits regally amid a horror-filled underworld flanked by her emblematic three-headed hound-snake-horse (she is governor of crossroads).

The chaste huntress

The spots on the Moon were thought by Romans to be forests where a lunar goddess hunted. Her Roman name is Diana (to the Greeks she was Artemis) and her women disciples were referred to as midnight revellers, depicted as a hoard of levitating women following the huntress as she rides her silver chariot through the night sky, firing silver bolts of moonlight back to Earth.

This ever-young huntress goddess has all the inconstancy one might associate with witches and the Moon. She is in essence contradictory. Like the hunter's arrow that takes life but also provides food and light, Diana is both fearsome killer and life-affirming protectress, fiercely chaste and yet patroness of childbirth. She has great affinity with wild animals (despite leading the hunt) and young girls, whom she protects until they marry, returning when they call her during childbirth to help alleviate pain and speed nature's progress. Yet she is the bringer of sudden death and illness to those same girls and women.

This goddess is renowned for being vengeful and blood-thirsty; she will kill on a whim and she rages. Artemis oversees women's lives during times of transition—not only childbirth, but puberty and death. These are times of fear, pain and loss as well as of creation and rebirth, and perhaps our anxiety is reflected in the goddess's nurturing yet frighteningly vengeful persona. She is a woman in a man's role, who seems to express the frustration and anger of the hunter who must put his life in danger to nurture an infant and her mother.

Artemis is known for her chasteness, and Diana became associated with the Christian protectress of women, children and mothers, the Virgin Mary, who took over her titles Queen of Heaven and Divine Virgin. The Blessed Virgin was linked with the Moon and the stars in the book of Revelation and in many depictions she wears a crown of twelve stars and floats upon a crescent Moon placed beneath her feet. In Portugal, one might address the Moon as Mother of God—in France Moon and Mary are *Notre Dame*—and to celebrate Mary, there is a tradition of baking moon cakes at Full Moon. In the 13th century, St. Anthony of Padua claimed this was her time because, like the Virgin, it is "in every way perfect", dispelling the darkness and promising the fullness of eternal life. The Moon that brought us the devilish, sexually fulfilled witch also gives us her opposite, the Holy Virgin and Mother of God.

"And there appeared a great wonder in Heaven; a woman clothed with the Sun, and the Moon under her feet, and upon her head a crown of twelve stars."

THE REVELATION OF ST. JOHN THE DIVINE

"From her immortal head a radiance is shown from Heaven and embraces Earth; and great is the beauty that ariseth from her shining light. The air, unlit before, glows with the light of her golden crown, and her rays beam clear, whensoever bright Selene [the Moon] having bathed her lovely body in the waters of Okeanos, and donned her far-gleaming raiment, and yoked her strong-necked, shining team, and drives on her long-maned horses at full speed, at eventime in the mid-month: then her great orbit is full and then her beams shine brightest as she increases. So she is a sure token and a sign to mortal men."

HOMERIC HYMN 32 TO SELENE **(c.7TH–4TH CENTURY BCE)**

TRANS. HUGH G. EVELYN-WHITE

right: ***Diana on her Chariot*, Albert Henry Payne, Date unknown, British**
Diana, or Selene, is often depicted, as here in this engraving, Payne after Correggio, wearing a circlet formed from a crescent moon which resembles a bow pulled taut, as if ready for the hunter to strike her prey.

Well met by moonlight

The witches' *sabbat* was considered, in continental Europe, at least, the focus of their unhallowed night-time revels. Witches were reputed to meet in bands of 13—a coven—at the Full Moon or on a Friday, the day on which their powers were thought particularly acute. So powerful was this belief that on Fridays in Germany church bells were said to strike the hour to release those who had been bewitched by their spells. Friday is the day most associated with goddess worship. In the Norse tradition, it was Freyja's day (she named the day in English); in ancient Greece it was the day of Aphrodite Salacia (she gave her name to salacious activity), who was depicted as a fish goddess, hence the eating of fish on Fridays and the association of sabbats with orgies (the fish has a long history as a symbol of fertility).

Sabbats were said to be addressed by the devil (events that parodied the religious services of the Christian sabbath) and also featured riotous dancing, with the devil leading the tune, perhaps on pipe or fiddle. The usual social conventions were turned on their head as partners danced back to back or hip to hip and made their circles "widdershins", counter-clockwise, or against the movement of the Sun, considered a very ill omen. The sabbats of lore were also fiercely sexual, the dancing often ending in coupling with monstrous nocturnal creatures, demons, or sometimes the devil himself, in the form of a goat, or a goat composite with bird's claws best served by a kiss on his second face (beneath the tail). At these night-time meetings, witches would gorge on rich food—English witches often confessed to eating dairy produce and smoked goods, which, in an era of poverty, constituted the best nourishment a mother could provide for her family.

Dishes might be brought to sabbats by familiars, or pulled in by the witches on ropes. Those who knew better knew not to eat, however hollow their stomachs: since it was the devil's food, which might turn to dust or dung. As we know from fairy lore, one should never trust supernatural food, which can entrap the greedy and the unaware in an otherworld forever.

Though the accounts of sabbats told in witch's confessions are compelling, there is no good historical evidence to suggest that organized covens of witches existed, by day or night, in the era when witchcraft trials were at their peak. Even inquisitors failed to find physical evidence of them and concluded that the confessions of "witches" were delusions or forced by torture. Today, groups of women do meet by night, whether to reclaim the streets, walk by the Moon or celebrate nature, using this "sabbath" time to retreat from the busy everyday world for a few hours and reflect on matters of the spirit.

following page: ***Midsummer Night in Sweden*, Allers Familj-Journal, 1918, Swedish**

While older witches stir a potion in a cauldron, younger members of a coven raise the spirits with a breathless circle dance.

"...as soon as the Sun sets they assemble in orchards of plum trees, or among ancient ruins, while on summer nights they hold their revels in barns, old hollow trees, by dark hedges or in subterranean caverns.... When a wild wind is blowing the witches love dearly to dance. Then they whirl about in eddying figures and capers, and when the sweat falls from them woe to the man who treads upon it!—for he will become at once dumb or lame, and may be called lucky should he escape with only an inflammation of the lungs."

GYPSY SORCERY AND FORTUNE-TELLING, CHARLES GODFREY LELAND

Hallowe'en

There are four great sabbat meetings in the year—Hallowe'en (31 October), Imbolc Eve (2 February), Walpurgis Night (31 April) and Lughnasadh (31 July), the herald, respectively of the new year/winter, summer, spring and harvest seasons. They are held on the evening before the new season starts: before new life begins there must be a celebration to mark the death of the old. These are considered "liminal" times, when the year passes from one state into another and the doors between realms are held ajar for a few hours of darkness. Spirits might travel over thresholds in either direction before the door shuts again with the dawn when order is restored.

Marking the end of the summer months and the seeming death of the Sun is Samhaim, or Hallowe'en. This is most important festival in the witch's calendar, celebrating the coming of the dark half of the year and the time when the curtain between the worlds is at its thinnest. Those born on this day are thought to have second sight or the power to communicate with spirits. For all who follow the Goddess, she changes form this evening. The voluptuous mother is replaced by the crone, an old woman of power who has mystery, magic, and tricks, at her fingertips. She's on our streets in a very tangible form in pre-teens dressed in pointy hats grasping buckets of candy and their older sisters parading dominatrix-inspired outfits. The church calendar has tied its own festivals to this older celebration: All Hallow's or All Saints' Day on November 1 is followed by All Soul's Day, a time to remember souls departed in the last year.

We might hold celebratory parties to mark Hallowe'en, with wine, song, feasting, merry-making and a period of quiet reflection on those lost recently and over the generations. But the most popular way to celebrate is with fire. Around the globe, we build bonfires and beacons, roll blazing barrels down hills, swing fireballs into the sky, carve lanterns and process with torches or place lights at the threshold to keep spirits at bay and augur the returning of the light. Hallowe'en fires were thought to bring succor to souls in purgatory and keep away evil: the wicked smile of the jack-o-lantern carved into a turnip, or more often a pumpkin, reflects, absorbs or scares off those with evil intent. Guising, or dressing up in order to blend in with the supernatural world, is another way to keep dangerous spirits at bay and pay them respect, perhaps all the better to communicate with them in the year to come.

Going "a-souling" is the Hallowe'en tradition of gathering offerings for the souls of the departed. Soulers would tour homes, knocking on doors and begging for sweet treats, silver or a sip of ale in exchange for merry-making and music. Today children carry on the tradition in the trick-or-treat spree. For Hallowe'en, like all witchy celebrations, is one of the days of the year when mischief-making is tolerated; when the uncanny is abroad, a little mortal madness makes no difference.

“Hey-how for Hallowe’en!
When all the witches are to be seen,
Some in black and some in green,
Hey-how for Hallowe’en!”

SCOTTISH RHYME

right: **Hallowe’en Postcard, Artist unknown, 1910, American**

A group of hags engage in a circle dance around a jack-o’-lantern under the merry gaze of the Moon. Sprites, ghosts and witches slip through the thinned membrane between our world and theirs on All Hallow’s Eve. The Hag has gathered very many powers over her good number of years and on this night she allows us to play with them in trick-or-treat or fortune-telling games.

Walpurgis night

Named in the Christian calendar after St. Walburga, an 8th-century nun who spoke out against witchcraft, this is the night before summer —the light half of the year—comes in. While dawn on the first day of May marks the beginning of great carousing, drinking and licentiousness (Beltane is a fertility celebration), the night before is more sinister. In the last few hours of darkness in the dark half of the year, however, anything might happen. Celebrations begin at the threshold of the day, at midnight, and mirror those of Hallowe'en, with carnivalesque parties, fires and trickery (from sprites and mischievous mortals alike). Indeed, this sabbat sits directly opposite Hallowe'en on the wheel of the witch's year. Tonight spirits are abroad, riding the skies in a vast, cacophonous train of fearsome winds, rain and supernatural ne'er-do-wells. Witches join them, taking to the sky on animals, pitchforks and new-made broomsticks. Mortals may join in, too, if feeling fearless; the best parties, so the legend goes, are held on wild mountain tops. More timid souls are advised to bar the doors and hang protective horseshoes and boughs of greenery over the threshold. Ringing bells, blowing whistles and clattering pans or singing spring songs (very loudly and en masse) can help, too. If you would like to meet a witch, this is the night: hang about at a crossroads, put on your clothes inside out, and have a few drinks too many (in most places that celebrate—northern Europe, Scandinavia and the Baltic regionÈthe following day is a public holiday).

But one of the most highly charged places to celebrate this "other Hallowe'en" may be Brocken in Germany, the highest peak of the Harz Mountains (you might hike there on the HarzerHexen Steig, the Harz

Witches Trail, which begins in Osterode in Lower Saxony). It is on this bare, high mountaintop, in Goethe's story *Faust*, on this night that the devilish Mephistopheles brings Faust to consort with witches awaiting the arrival of spring. Indeed, in Germany, the night may be referred to as *Hexennacht*, witches night, when just as at Hallowe'en, children dress as witches, teenagers get up to anti-social mischief, and unhinged madness is not only tolerated, but expected.

previous page: ***Salem Witch on her Broom*, Artist unknown, *c.* 1925, American**

A witch flies by night on her broomstick accompanied by her familiar, a black cat, over the town of Salem, Massachusetts on this postcard from the last century.

following page: ***Walpurgis Night*, Wood engraving after drawing by Franz Simm, 1880–1890, Austrian**

Illustration from the *Works of Goethe*, *Faust* Part 1 where Mephistopheles brings Faust to consort with the witches in Walpurgis madness.

"Once a year comes Free-night. Yes, truly, Free-night. Then the witches, laughing scornfully, ride to Blocksberg, upon the mountain-top, on their broomsticks, the same broomsticks with which at other times their witchcraft is whipped out of them, then the whole wild company skims along the forest way, and then the wild desires awaken in our hearts which life has not fulfilled."

THE BOOK OF HALLOWE'EN, RUTH EDNA KELLEY

Creatures of the night

Witches exchange form or hang out with many "Moon-familiars", nocturnal creatures including the owl, hare, cat, fox, toad and snail. The hare looms especially large in folk tales, where it often becomes a witch's alter-ego. Folklorists through the ages hear stories about hunters out by night chasing an elusive hare. When one finally hits his prey, the animal escapes and the hunters trail it to a house in the forest or on the hill, where it disappears.

> *...the witch put on her bonnet and coat, and started. Her husband watched her from their cottage door, down the hill; and at the bottom of the hill, he saw his wife quietly place herself on the ground and disappear. In her place a fine hare ran on at its full speed.*

Next day, the granny or wife who lives there is found with a wound in the self-same place that the hare took the shot. It is said in India that one can see a hare in the Moon when it's waxing, from around the eighth day after New Moon to the Full Moon. Taoist tales tell that the hare in the Moon is employed by a genii to pound up the potions that form the elixir of life. The hare certainly displays an intoxicating life-force: it is known for its leaping, is super-fertile and has moments of ecstatic madness. In her mad March hare rituals, the doe stands on her back

right: *Jade Hare*, Yoshitoshi, 1889, Japanese

By the light of the Full Moon, the monkey who stole and ate the peaches of longevity dances with the Jade Hare, who lives on the Moon. This is a popular legend in China and Japan.

月百姿
玉兎
孫悟空

legs to box, fighting off the advances of a predatory male. Since the hare is considered as powerful as a witch, it is thought to be especially unlucky to see one when pregnant or heading off to sea. Even today this is the animal that no seafarer dare name, though thanks to sympathetic magic, carrying its foot may guard against attack by witchcraft.

The night-crawling toad is held in particular awe around the world for fear that it might be a witch in another skin—the term for toad in many Romany dialects is said to be the same as the word "devil". Those who find a toad in the home might throw her on a fire to negate her supernatural influence; equally, she might be treated with respect to court her powers. This is a creature of transformation that moves between worlds in its journey from tadpole to toad, and is said to bring back prophesies from its forays, including its trips to the Moon. Native American and Chinese legends describe a toad in the moon, and the creature was sacred to the Greek lunar goddess of the underworld, Hecate.

In a web of lore that extends from the Celtic world to China, toads have been associated with witches because of the psychotropic potential of their skin secretions. Like the magic mushroom, toad secretions can bring about states of ecstasy or paralysis that might give a sensation of flying. The toad is also associated, like the witch, with erotic passion and control of a woman's fertility—there was a widespread belief in parts of Europe and Africa that the toad was responsible for pregnancy. Toad effigies or preserved parts of the creature might be used as fertility charms or a magic "bone" (that reputedly appears after ants have picked over a dead toad) used in powerful love charms or as a surrogate love-magic doll for sticking with pins. The toad was believed also to have a precious jewel in its head, which, when extracted and worn, preserved pregnant women from supernatural ills and cured bites and stings.

The Toad-Maid

Thus it happened to a youth of Aramsach, near Kattenberg, that, being one day in a lonely place by a lake, there looked up at him from the water a being somewhat like a maid but more like a hideous toad, with whom he entered into conversation; which became at last friendly and agreeable, for the strange creature talked exceeding well. Then she, thinking he might be hungry, asked him if he would fain have anything in particular to eat. He mentioned in jest a kind of cakes; whereupon, diving into the lake, she brought some up, which he ate. So he met her many times; and whenever he wished for anything, no matter what, she got it for him from the waters: the end of it all being that, despite her appalling ugliness, the youth fell in love with her and offered marriage, to which she joyfully consented. But no sooner had the ceremony been performed than she changed to a lady of wonderful beauty; and, taking him by the hand, she conducted him to the lake, into which she led him, and in this life they were seen never more.

***GYPSY SORCERY AND FORTUNE TELLING*, CHARLES GODFREY LELAND**

The weird sisters

The dark atmosphere and supernatural spectacle at the beginning of Shakespeare's play *Macbeth* is provided by three hags, who meet by night on a "blasted" heath to make spells. It is as if *their* incantations, not the words of the playwright, which conjure up the drama that follows. Nameless and shrouded in darkness, these crones are scarcely recognizable as human; on first spying them, Banquo asks,

> *What are these*
> *So withered and so wild in their attire,*
> *That look not like the inhabitants o' the earth.*
> *And yet are on't?*

Like the audience, he knows not whether they are real or fantastic, woman or man, with their "choppy" fingers, skinny lips and beards. Disconcertingly—for modern and contemporary audiences alike—the witches well played by men (boys usually filled female parts), and this convention was followed into the 19th century, when comedic actors generally took the parts. One viewer, Fanny Kemble, wrote somewhat disparagingly of a production in 1833: "We have three jolly-faced fellows, whom we are accustomed to laugh at...with a due proportion of petticoats...jocose red faces, peaked hats, and broomsticks."

However crummy the acting, the sisters bind Macbeth with their spell-casting and fortune-telling. Audiences might interpret the torments that terrorize the would-be king as being of the hags' making —his inability to sleep, the terrible dreams that shake him nightly, the dark, "cursed thoughts" that wrack his conscience. What are his hallucinations—the "air-drawn dagger" and ghost of Banquo—but an expression of their control over his destiny, like the control they exert over the forces of nature when thunder and lightning crackle as they take the stage.

The stagey sensationalism of the weird sisters, the comedic grotesqueness of the substances they stir into their cauldron, from eye of bat to "finger of birth-strangled babe", seems to hint at the conclusion modern audiences may reach. That though the macabre acts of the play are prompted by the witches' prophesies and spell-making, they are made flesh by Macbeth's own dark weaknesses—his fascination with the things no mortal should know, and his ability to switch off his morality: "To know my deed 'twere best not to know myself", he tells us. The acts are propelled to their conclusion by the moral weaknesses of his wife, perhaps the most credibly drawn witch in the play to modern minds. With her we even witness the creation of the stereotypical witch, as she calls up the dark spirits to suckle at her breast:

Come to my woman's breasts,
And take my milk for gall, your murdering ministers,
Wherever in your sightless substances
You wait on nature's mischief!

Making a covenant with the forces of evil will give her the dark energy she and her husband need to accomplish the dreadful murders at the heart of the story.

Darkness and blood

Interview with Sîan Thomas

One of Britain's most accomplished stage and screen actors, Siân Thomas has appeared in numerous productions for the Citizens' Theatre Company, the National Theatre and the Royal Shakespeare Company (RSC). She won the TMA Martini Award for Best Supporting Actress for *Uncle Vanya* and was nominated for a 2003 Olivier Award for her performance in *Up For Grabs*. Her recent feature films include *Harry Potter and the Order of the Phoenix* and *Vanity Fair*, in which she stars alongside Reese Witherspoon and James Purefoy. Here, she discusses her interpretation of Lady Macbeth in the 2004 RSC production, which explored the vulnerability and tenderness at the heart of a character often thought of as witch-like in her capacity to do evil.

Lady Macbeth is a challenging role.

Lady Macbeth is a role I've always wanted to play because she's such a conundrum. She is one of Shakespeare's great and challenging characters. It's such a famous part and so many famous people have

previous page: *Macbeth and the Three Witches*, Boydell, late 18th century, British

Macbeth comes across the prophesying weird sisters in this engraving from Boydell's *Shakespeare*. The three are surrounded by visions of his future—murdered infants and the ghostly forms of kings—as well as symbols of their craft, including creatures of the night.

played her in so many different ways. Most of all, I was keen to get away from the cliché of an icy, evil queen with a heart of stone, who plucks babies from her nipples and dashes out their brains because the point is that she hasn't done anything of the kind. What she says is that she would do that if she had to, because she cares so deeply. Dominic Cooke (the director) and I agree that she's a human being who does know how tender it is to love the babe. Her will is powerful and she knows what she wants. When she summons up the spirits, she does so, not because she's full of dire cruelty, but because she needs the assistance of supernatural powers.

What does Lady Macbeth want?

Lady Macbeth wants power. She wants to be queen but she can only do that through her husband. Nowadays, a character like Lady Macbeth would have a high-powered creative job.... Instead, she lives in an utterly masculine world in which women are powerless, in which their sole function is to procreate. She clearly has had a child but the child has died. We decided that the baby was Macbeth's, rather than a child from a previous marriage, which means there is always the ghost of a child between them—a fact made more terrible because they need an heir. Their name can only live on through their children and they have none.

The key for me was Lady Macbeth's line "I have given suck, and know/How tender 'tis to love the babe that milks me" (I.vii.54–55). She does have a tenderness: she has known tenderness. And yet she wants to do this terrible thing. Murdering the king is so important to her, her life depends on it, she's invested so much in it that she would actually be prepared to commit an appalling act and pluck a baby from her nipple and dash out its brains. So there are two opposing characteristics: there's a woman who's capable of planning dreadful deeds and at the same time capable of passion and tenderness.

Tell us about her dark energy.

The minute Lady Macbeth has read Macbeth's letter [telling of the witches' prophesy for him] she thinks, "Yes! Yes! We can do it. It's easy. Everything will be fine." There's a wonderful expression that Nietzsche used to describe a dark, exultant energy: "strong pessimism". You stand on the abyss and instead of looking down and thinking "Help, I'm scared! I don't want to jump" you just think "Yeah, I'll jump and to hell with it: If we've got to go, let's go blazing." It's a life force, a dark energy but nevertheless an alive, passionate thing. I think Lady Macbeth has strong pessimism. Macbeth hasn't so much, because his mind, his imagination, stops him. There's also a vulnerability about her, for example when she says "Had he not resembled/My father as he slept, I had done't" (II.ii.12–13). The fact that the sleeping Duncan resembles her father shakes her profoundly. So there's a double edge and you have to decide whether to go for one thing very strongly or perhaps, more interestingly, hold the two opposite reins in your hands and see if you can show both, because it's a shame if you reduce a part to black and white. As [legendary Shakespearean director] John Barton says, look for the grey areas and play them.

Where does this dark energy lead her?

When we first meet Lady Macbeth she wants, she needs something to come into her life because she's a bit fed up and depressed. And then she gets Macbeth's letter and suddenly she's in control and she says "let's go for it—let's murder him". But by the end of the play, from being a passionate creature, she's reduced to two big terrors: darkness and blood. She's in the dark, dreaming of blood and it destroys her. She has opened Pandora's box, created Frankenstein's monster, unleashed chaos and as a result, she loses control.

I hope our audiences, many of whom will be teenagers, will leave the theatre having understood the story and seen that the Macbeths are real people, not strange, evil, fairy creatures. I hope everyone in the audience, regardless of age, will see that the Macbeths are people of flesh and blood who commit dreadful acts, just as real people do, because I think that what Shakespeare is saying is that we are all Macbeth, we are all capable of being human.... It's not a happy play but, like all great tragedies, it is oddly uplifting. We see where Macbeth goes wrong and should be able to recognize that we too might well have done the same thing. The play can teach us much about humanity and therefore more about ourselves.

Black as night

Women accused of being witches in the early modern period probably didn't dress differently from other women, though they may have looked a little less well-kempt, since they tended to be poorer and many were accused of bad housekeeping. Some witness statements say that witches chose clothing of red and green, which have supernatural associations in fairy lore. Some even describe witches dressing like fairies. But to modern eyes, witches are synonymous with black gowns and pointy hats.

Lawyers have worn black since early modern times, linking their sombre gowns with great intelligence and the art of prediction and foretelling right from wrong. But in Western culture, black is more often associated with darkness, the forces of the underworld (it denotes mourning) and evil. The blackness of a witch's outfit seems to connect her with a legendary dark age long ago, before we were enlightened and when people were unreasoning, an idea common to fairy lore. Wearing black points towards the confident sexuality of the little black dress and the dominatrix. But above all, black denotes otherness, often defining people outside mainstream society. In the 1970s, female punks were attacked in the street for wearing black; today Muslim women wearing the all-covering black *jilhab*—a public declaration of faith and modesty that seems to intimidate politicians and headteachers—may be attacked with the word "witch" or worse.

What of the iconic witch's hat? It resembles the headgear worn by Welsh women in "national dress", which Nathaniel Hawthorn wrote in 1854, "makes them look ugly and witch-like". The Welsh "chimney" hat, just one of a variety of hats worn in different regions over

hundreds of years, was steered toward its iconic status by the English-born Lady Llanover, keen to preserve a distinct dress for each region, as well as support the Welsh language and flannel industry. The style appeared first in the 1840s, an amalgamation of a man's top hat and earlier country headgear, and was picked up as a distinctive Welsh image by a burgeoning tourist industry keen to market souvenir postcards and prints.

The iconography of the pointy-hatted witch seems to have stuck fairly late, and only in Western Europe and the United States. Before the 19th century, witches wore all manner of headgear—or were typified by an indecent lack of head-covering. Even in Germany until recently, the witch has worn an old woman's headscarf. In Europe in the Middle Ages, witches were often depicted in the headgear and everyday clothes of the Waldensians, an order of Christians in France, Switzerland, Austria and Italy who led an abstemious life preaching the Gospel to the poor. They were excommunicated in 1184 and, after torture, admitted to moonlight sabbats in the woods, and the use of hallucinogens and self-pleasuring rods.

Some suggest that the hat's point hints at the devil's horns or resembles hats won by Quakers or Jews, enemies of the established church. Other sources say that pointed hats, the height of sophistication for urbanites in 16th and 17th-century Europe, were later worn only by rural peasants, and so became a byword for backwardness. However, ancient Etruscan coins depict the lunar goddess Diana wearing a conical hat, and great golden cone-shaped headgear engraved with Sun and Moon symbols has been unearthed in central Europe; scholars suggest they may have been worn by wizards and magi some 3,300 years ago. In 2006, excavations of a

3,000-year-old "Celtic" tomb on the Silk Road in western China found the preserved body of a woman. Her face and comb were adorned with magical-looking symbols, and she held a *sheila-na-gig*, icon of the crone goddess. On her head she wore a perfectly preserved tall, conical hat.

"secret, black and midnight hags"

***MACBETH*, WILLIAM SHAKESPEARE**

previous page: ***Jacobean Tea*, Photographer unknown, early 20th century, British**

Though often mistaken for Welsh ladies taking tea, these women were in fact photographed in the English county of Norfolk. They wear Jacobean dress, as is the tradition at their almshouses, the Hospital of Holy and Undivided Trinity at Castle Rising, Norfolk. The hospital was established in 1610 to house 20 spinsters of "good character". "No common beggar, harlot, scold or drunkard" was admitted entry.

Night's black agents

In Macbeth, Banquo uses the term "instruments of darkness" to sum up the role of the hags; they are not the devil, but do his work in human form. King James I, writing in his *Daemonologie*, declared that while the devil himself appears to mighty magicians, witches and other lesser practitioners of the dark arts are content to consort with demons in the likeness of dogs or apes, rats, ferrets or crows. King James goes on to say that these servants of the devil only approach a would-be witch when she is on her own, perhaps when working in the fields, walking through a forest or in bed—and that he only chooses those open to his advances: atheists and women who curse or blaspheme. In Elizabeth Sawyer's confession of 1621, the "Divell" is reported to say to her, on hearing her take the Lord's name in vain, "Oh! have I now found you cursing, swearing, and blaspheming? now you are mine."

In return for the use of her body and soul, the demon, in whichever form he appears, offers the witch a reward—fortune perhaps, her heart's desire, a rich feast or wealthy husband—or to "vex" the "bodies" and beasts towards whom she feels malice, envy or anger. Alternatively, he might threaten to tear her to pieces, and she, "soore feared", agrees to a pact to send him on his way. Once agreed, infernal covenants are sealed with blood; most often the demon sucks from a teat near the witch's "privy parts". The demon would subsequently appear at unexpected times, commanding his victim to do ill, or asking how he might assuage her rage or envy. Such women were not actively worshipping the devil, more succumbing to their own evil feelings by proxy.

It was thought that women were especially open to the devil's influence because of their distracting bodies and melancholic disposition, and witches were able to redirect him onto the unsuspecting. Demonic possession was an affliction of sweet young girls, such as those at Salem, or of nuns—and its signs were spectacular. Pious angels suffered raging seizures, their heads turned backward and emitted rasping or gruff voices, they spoke foreign or liturgical languages and engaged in complex theological arguments. The possessed displayed the strength of a prize-fighter and a knowledge of sexual matters far beyond their years or moral standing. What else could this be but the work of witches?

If the devil was rather late arriving on the scene—previously, he was one among a pantheon of invisible spirits, from ghosts to fairies and ogres—by the 17th century he had become one of the defining features of the supernatural world. The church invented Satan and introduced him to witches, wedding his form to demons of folklore, like the incubus and succubus, to forge connections between sorcery and heresy. Having an extreme force of evil on which to pin misfortune may have held appeal in the second half of the 16th century, a chaotic time of anxiety about climate change, religious conflict, warfare and social upheaval.

Today, the devil's work remains the stuff of the church. Though outsiders commonly link modern witchcraft with satanic worship, the devil and Wiccans don't meet. Since he's a construct of Christianity, Satan can't be part of the pagan world, which does not recognize absolute evil. Modern witches understand that the world is shaded not in demonic black and angelic white, but in an infinite number of tones between.

“They sacrifice to demons, adore them, seek out and accept responses from them, do homage to them, and make them a written agreement or another kind of pact through which, by a single word, touch or sign, they may perform whatever evil deeds or sorcery they wish and be transported to or away from wherever they wish…”

LETTER FROM POPE EUGENIUS IV **(1437)**

right: ***A Horned Witch*****, French School, date unknown, French**

The sitter’s idiosyncratic hairstyle, pointed headdress and black clothing direct modern viewers to the conclusion that she is a witch, but her beauty, measured countenance and gentle gaze confound our expectations.

The Terror Of Possession

The Sin of Witchcraft. We read about it, we look on it from the outside; but we can hardly realize the terror it induced. Every impulsive or unaccustomed action, every little nervous affection, every ache or pain was noticed, not merely by those around the sufferer, but by the person himself, whoever he might be, that was acting, or being acted upon, in any but the most simple and ordinary manner. He or she (for it was most frequently a woman or girl that was the supposed subject) felt a desire for some unusual kind of food—some unusual motion or rest—her hand twitched, her foot was asleep, or her leg had the cramp; and the dreadful question immediately suggested itself, "Is any one possessing an evil power over me; by the help of Satan?" and perhaps they went on to think, "It is bad enough to feel that my body can be made to suffer through the power of some unknown evil-wisher to me; but what if Satan gives them still further power, and they can touch my soul, and inspire me with loathful thoughts leading me into crimes which at present I abhor?" and so on, till the very dread of what might happen, and the constant dwelling of the thoughts, even with horror, upon certain possibilities, or what were esteemed such, really brought about the corruption of imagination at last, which at first they had shuddered at. Moreover, there was a sort of uncertainty as to who might be infected—not unlike the overpowering dread of the plague, which made some shrink from their best-beloved with irrepressible fear. The brother or sister, who was the dearest friend of their childhood and youth, might now be bound in some mysterious deadly pact with evil spirits of the most horrible kind—who could tell?

***LOIS THE WITCH*, ELIZABETH GASKELL**

"There was an old granny who lost her sight,
Cold lies the Dew.
She couldn't tell if it were morning or night,
Cold lies the Dew.
There come a fine gentleman, black as a coal,
'I'll give 'ee some eyes, if you'll sell me your soul,'
Cold lies the Dew."

ANON BALLAD

Night rider

The phenomenon of the "nightmare", or being hag-ridden, has been observed from Europe to the Far East. One awakes suddenly, terrified from a delirious dream but paralyzed, unable to cry out or even take a breath and pinned down by a dreadful pressure on the chest. That suffocating weight is the hag, squatting on the chest. Some describe a sound that accompanies the sensation, like the padding of a cat or rodent crossing the floor. The phenomenon, linked to a syndrome referred to as "sudden death with structurally normal heart", was most vividly portrayed in Fuseli's highly charged painting "*The Nightmare*" (1781), where the crushing spirit is pictured in the forms of a demon and a spectral mare assaulting a Hammer Horror-style wench (see pages 72–73). So awful is men's fear of the night hag that men in Thailand have been reported to go to bed wearing lipstick, to fool her.

"To go a-horsing" is a derogatory term coined in ancient Greece for sexually insatiable women, and this nightmare is but one step from the incubus (male) and succubus (female) spirits who first incapacitate and then molest those who sleep, either with erotic dreams that become horror movies just before climax, or by shifting from comely woman to beast or alien sex fiend. This skill of the night hag is echoed in the daylight witch's art of paralysis. In the St. Osyth witchcraft trial of 1582, one witness claimed that he and his cart were charmed still for more than one hour, unable to move forward or back. In the Brothers' Grimm tale *Jorinde and Joringel*, any man who comes within one hundred paces of the witch's castle finds that he can "neither weep nor speak, nor move hand or foot" until the witch has had her way and bids him be free.

A suspected witch was often reported to leave an effigy in bed with her husband while she flew off on her night-ridings. From the late 16th century we hear of a man accusing his wife of being a witch on the evidence that she was absolutely still in bed, without seeming to breathe, and could not be roused by shaking for two or more hours "until the cock crowed", when she suddenly awoke. If such women did not ride a broom on this night flight, they might borrow a horse to ride into the ground. It would collapse on return just before dawn, sweating, exhausted and near collapse, a state known as "hag-ridden".

The Witch Wife

A cabinetmaker in Bühl slept in a bed in his workshop. Several nights in a row something laid itself onto his chest and pressed against him until he could hardly breathe. After talking the matter over with a friend, the next night he lay awake in bed. At the stroke of 12 a cat slipped in through a hole. The cabinetmaker quickly stopped up the hole, caught the cat, and nailed down one of its paws. Then he went to sleep. The next morning he found a beautiful naked woman in the cat's place. One of her hands was nailed down. She pleased him so much that he married her. One day, after she had borne him three children, she was with him in his workshop, when he said to her, "Look, that is where you came in!" and he opened the hole that had been stopped up until now. The woman suddenly turned into a cat, ran out through the opening and she was never seen again.

VOLKSSAGEN AUS DEM LANDE BADEN UND DEN ANGRENZENDEN GEGENDEN,

BERNHARD BAADER

A witch bearing gifts

One old crone who tiptoes into the bedroom by night resembles the fairy godmother more than the night hag. This is La Befana, the old witch who brings presents to good Italian children as they sleep on 5 January, Epiphany Eve, the night before the three kings are said to have arrived at the stable in Bethlehem. She is sweeping her home when three fine men arrive at her door, asking directions to the stable. She doesn't know the way and sends them on their way—she has so much cleaning to get through—but later regrets her decision and sets out to find the infant king, taking some of the toys once loved by her own dear departed child. She never reaches the stable. When at last she starts out, the kings are long gone, and though La Befana pursues every possible trail at every crossroads, and searches in every village and at every home where there is a child in the hope that the infant Jesus will be there, she cannot find him. Instead, she leaves toys for the good children, and for the disobedient deposits coal (today candy *coal*), garlic or switches from her broom.

The old woman has many of the attributes of a witch: she is wizened, wrinkled and melancholic—some versions of the tale have her almost depraved with grief, hallucinating about the death of her infant and sure the Christ child is hers. She has lived alone since the death of her husband and infant child. Her anxieties about housekeeping and the kings' status are her downfall, just as small misunderstandings about lost items, uncleanliness or respect marked out women as witches in earlier centuries. She sits astride a broom, dressed in black and sprinkled with soot (an ingredient of witch's ointment) carrying a hand-bell. Pealing bells is a sure way to scare off spirits with evil intent, and some say bells were once rung on Epiphany night to warn the world of her presence, for La Befana is ignorant of, or even doubts, the story of the birth of Christ.

Like Saint Nicholas, this witch is a spirit associated with the hearth —she too comes down the chimney unseen to fill the pockets of clothes or socks pinned to the mantlepiece, and she, like all supernatural spirits, is sighted not on the holy day itself, but on the preceding eve between midnight and dawn, the witching hours. Italian children might even refer to her as Mrs Santa. Folklorists connect her with the passing of the old year, when effigies of an old woman might be burned to extinguish the old and make space for the new. And so every year she begins her endless, two-thousand-year search anew; she never reaches the Child of Light, nor is absolved by his blessing.

previous page: ***The Nightmare*, Henry Fuseli, 1780s, Swiss**

***The Nightmare* conveys the full Gothic horror and erotic thrill of being hag-ridden or assaulted by an incubus. It caused a sensation from its first public exhibition in 1782.**

following page: ***Epiphany Puppets of La Befana*, Alessia Pierdomenico, 2005, Italian**

Puppets of "Mother Christmas", the hag Befana, wearing her signature headscarf on sale at Italian Christmas markets.

Ladies Of Epiphany

In early times the Feast of the Epiphany, which is the 13th day after Christmas Eve, was feared because at that time the three goddesses, Berchta, Holle and Befana, with their ghostly companions, were especially active, and, as a guard against their machinations, the initial letters of the names of the three kings or wise men, were written on many a door.

Of the trio, Berchta was represented as a shaggy monster, whose name was used as a bugbear with which to frighten children. She was intrusted with overseeing of spinning, and on the eve of Epiphany she visited the homes of the countryfolk, distributing empty reels, which she required to be filled within a specific time; if her demands were not met, she retaliated by tangling and befouling the flax.

Holle or Holde, was a benign and merciful goddess, of an obliging disposition, who was usually most lenient, except when she noticed disorder in the affairs of a household. Her favorite resorts were the lakes and fountains, but she would also oversee domestic concerns, and shared with Berchta the supervision of spinning. Sometimes, however, she appeared as an old hag, with bristling, matted hair and long teeth.

Befana, the third goddess, was of Italian origin, and her name signifies Epiphany. On that day the women and children used to place a rag doll in the window in her honor. In personal appearance she was black and ugly, but her disposition was not unfriendly.

***THE MAGIC OF THE HORSE-SHOE*, ROBERT MEANS LAWRENCE**

A parallel world

Interview with Jany Temime

French costume designer Jany Temime is best known for her accomplished work on the Harry Potter films, which began with the third instalment, *The Prisoner of Azkaban*. She has also provided costumes for stars including Renée Zellweger, Colin Firth, Hugh Grant, Minnie Driver, Rhys Ifans and Joseph Fiennes, and has worked on two Oscar-winning films, *Antonia's Line* and *Karakter*. She won the BAFTA Wales award for Best Costume Design for the movie *House of America*, and two Golden Calfs for Best Costume Design at Film Festival Utrecht for *Antonia's Line* and *The Partisans*.

You are redefining the notion of what a witch looks like for a new generation. How have you broken away from the concept of a witch in a pointy hat and black cloak?

That is a very stereotyped image; we are trying to pull the idea of a witch away from what we associate with the American Hallowe'en celebration. We like to make our witches as individual as possible—after all, the world of witches and warlocks in Harry Potter is a world that lies parallel to our world. We all wear clothes to reflect our personalities, and so do the characters in the films. There are a thousand ways of wearing a pointy hat, and everybody has her own way of being and looking witchy. Take the girls from the Beauxbâtons Academy of Magic in *Harry Potter and the Goblet of Fire*. They wear sophisticated outfits because they come from a very exclusive school for witches, perhaps in Paris. Other characters might dress in a more traditional or modest way, more like the idea of a witch from the 16th century, because that reflects their personality. Then there is Bellatrix Lestrange, who is dressed rather like a dominatrix because she is in love with the Dark Lord Voldemort, but she also has a form of hysteria which is reflected in her dress, and she wears a medieval-style costume because she is a Death Eater—all these creatures are medieval in dress.

As well as representing many centuries and social categories, the costumes in the Harry Potter films are as international as possible. We look to African and Bulgar traditions, for example, because the world of witches and wizards encompasses many cultures. We also like to show that though Hogwarts' School was founded over a thousand years ago, it continues to evolve, so the academic gown has evolved through the films. We must remember that the witch and wizarding world is always moving on, just like our own world.

chapter 2

Natural Magic

Awesome power

Witches are reputed to command the elements. Being so at one with nature, witches seem able to experience life fully; at an atomic level, where there is no division between person, animal, rock or planet. This transcendental state—being aware of the oneness of everything—is the stuff of enlightened beings, and is only attained in many religious traditions following years of sustained spiritual practice that often involves chanting words of power and adopting ecstatic body postures, both associated with witches.

So potent and uncanny is this semi-divine power in the hands of mortals that it can drive those who witness it insane. One Mother Arnold, a notorious witch with numerous pseudonyms and identities who was brought to trial in 1574, was seen "walking in water" by a mackerel fisherman. At the sight, the spirit entered him and he "fell mad", attempting to kill himself. When Macbeth notes, "So foul and fair a day I have not seen" before first encountering his witches, he already understands their ability to confound nature and confuse mankind.

previous page: ***Sorcery*, Howard Pyle, 1903, British**

right: **Mad Kate, Henry Fuseli, 1806–07, Swiss**

Mad Kate **perches barefoot on a rock as the storm rages all around, seeming to conduct the elements with her fingers. Hers are the eyes of one who sees beyond this world.**

Mucha

The sorceress Medea

Medea is the ancient world's most renowned sorceress. She learned her "exceeding skill" mixing drugs and words of wisdom as a priestess of Hecate, goddess of the underworld and patroness of witches, and used them to subdue dragons, restore the aged to youth, raise tempests and becalm seas. She uses these powers to benefit those she loves—for love of Jason, she blends magic ointments and wisely smoothes over his mortal failings to help him win the Golden Fleece. Along the way she has no compunction in betraying father and country to enable Jason to fulfil his destiny, and monstrously murders her brother to confound Jason's foes.

Jason might do well to take note. For those who cross her, Medea is more treacherous and vengeful still, and will stop at nothing to use her powers for ill. In Euripedes' play *Medea* (431 BCE), their nurse even has to warn the witch's children to beware "her savage mood, the fell tempest of her reckless heart". Medea and Jason settle in the city of Corinth, where Medea's powerful skills seem exotic and other, like her looks; she is quite out of place. Though they have children together, and Medea is the cause of Jason's good fortune and standing, he decides to take a new wife, not a savage creature such as she, but the daughter of the king of Corinth. With the forces of nature at her command and anguish in her heart at the thought of her husband lying by his new royal bride's side, there is nothing in Medea's "proud restless soul" that she is not capable of. She spins a wedding gown of poison; when the rays of the morning sun touch it, it burns like fire, consuming the flesh of the new bride and her father who tries to save her. This is not enough. Medea then slaughters her own children to spite their father. When accused of murder, the sorceress retorts that though it was not Jason's hand that killed them, it was his treachery; he did it. She makes a strong case and we empathize with the witch's distress, remaining on her side as she flees the scene on a magical golden chariot.

Medea is an archetypal witch not only for her magical knowledge and her mastery of the natural world, but for her willingness to voice and enact the vengeful feelings of wronged women everywhere. And because she can carry through the most unnatural act of all, the killing of her children—with her power over nature she is only too well equipped to carry out the greatest crime against nature.

previous page: ***The Invocation*, Alphonse Marie Mucha, 1897–99, French**

The sorceress sends up incense to the heavens with the swooning sounds of plucked strings. In return she calls down the powers of nature.

"Oft...I have...
Made clouds, or sunshine; tempests rise, or fall;
And stubborn lawless winds obey my call:
With mutter'd words disarm'd the viper's jaw;
Up by the roots vast oaks, and rocks cou'd draw,
Make forests dance, and trembling mountains come,
Like malefactors, to receive their doom;
Earth groan, and frightened ghosts forsake their tomb."

METAMORPHOSES, OVID (C.28 CE)

Storm-raising

In the winter months of 1589–90, King James I was bringing his Danish bride, Anne, home to Scotland when his fleet of ships was blown off course by severe winds and tempestuous rain. The king's "tempest-tost" vessel narrowly escaped the powerful winds and waves that wracked it on all sides. Blame for the storm was pinned on a group of women, known thereafter as the North Berwick Witches, one of whom confessed that they had sailed out to sea in sieves and riddles to drown a cat with various parts of dead men strapped to it (a traditional way to raise a violent sea storm) before taking hands to dance a reel into the church. King James invited the women to replicate the dance at their trial, and to which he "tooke great delight", as if it were a theatrical performance.

Storm witches have been renowned since classical times; ancient Greek and Roman literature tells of their power to draw up rain and tempest by peeing, stirring a pool of water in violent circles, and combing or shaking out their locks. In coastal regions, rocky outcrops are said to be haunted by legendary witches, renowned for bringing in storms to wreck ships. And at ports, weather women would wait to do magic for sailors setting out to sea. Using a rope or handkerchief, they could arrange for the winds to do the sailors' bidding—for a price. One form of wind-charming involved sound magic: whirling a piece of wood attached to a length of string around the head until its whirring produced wind sounds that varied in tone. But far more common was a knotted talisman that served as a charm of protection and could be undone to unleash the winds when becalmed. The usual trick, written about since the 14th century, was to tie three knots: when the first was undone, it unleashed a gentle breeze from the south; the second brought a "mackerel gale" from the north; and the last knot held a hurricane. The Lapps and Finns were considered mistresses of the trade.

The witch's knot also functioned as a protective symbol and could be inscribed over doors to safeguard animal and mortal inhabitants. The knot motif gained its power by representing four winds, which were drawn—in one stroke—as four vesica piscis shapes gathered north, east, south and west around a central circle, which might represent both the globe of the Earth and a magic place of protection. The vesica piscis is an ancient sign of female power and fecundity since it resembles both the vulva and the fish, famed for its abundance of eggs. Knot magic was an offence against the state across Europe from as early as the 6th century, since its methods could be employed in tying curses. A common type involved inserting the black feathers of magical birds, such as raven, into the knots, to create the much-feared witch's ladder or garland.

"When shall we three meet again In thunder, lightning, or in rain?"

***MACBETH*, WILLIAM SHAKESPEARE**

following page: ***Macbeth and the Witches*, Joseph Anton Koch, 1834, Austrian**

In Koch's painting, the three hags are cast as sea witches. They have drawn up a storm and a phantom army of mounted warriors descends from the clouds.

Seat of Storms

On the top [of a sheer face of cliff] is placed a stone of somewhat remarkable shape, which is by no great effort of the imagination converted into a chair. There it was that Madgy Figgy...was in the habit of seating herself when she desired to call up to her aid the spirits of the storm. Often has she been seen swinging herself to and fro on this dizzy height when a storm has been coming home upon the shores, and richly laden vessels have been struggling with the winds. From this spot she poured forth her imprecations on man and beast, and none whom she had offended could escape those withering spells; and from this chair, which will ever bear her name, Madgy Figgy would always take her flight. Often, starting like some huge bird, mounted on a stem of ragwort, Figgy has headed a band of inferior witches, and gone off rejoicing in their iniquities to Wales or Spain.

This old hag lived in a cottage not far from Raftra, and she and her gang, who appear to have been a pretty numerous crew, were notorious wreckers. On one occasion, Magdy from her seat of storms lured a Portuguese Indiaman into Perloe Cove, and drowned all the passengers. As they were washed on shore, the bodies were stripped of everything valuable, and buried by Figgy and her husband in the green hollow, which may yet be seen just above Perloe Cove, marking the graves with a rough stone placed at the head of the corpse. The spoils on this occasion must have been large, for all the women were supplied for years with rich dresses, and costly jewels were seen decking the red arms of the girls who laboured in the fields. For a long time gems and gold continued to be found on the sands.

Howbeit, amongst the bodies thrown ashore was one of a lady richly dressed, with chains of gold about her. "Rich and rare were the gems she wore," and not only so, but valuable treasure was fastened around her, she evidently hoping, if saved, to secure some of her property. This body, like all the others, was stripped; but Figgy said there was a mark on it which boded them evil, and she would not allow any of the gold or gems to be divided, as it would be sure to bring bad luck if it were separated. A dreadful quarrel ensued, and bloodshed was threatened; but the diabolical old Figgy was more than a match for any of the men, and the power of her impetuous will was superior to them all.

Everything of value, therefore, belonging to this lady was gathered into a heap, and placed in a chest in Madgy Figgy's hut. They buried the Portuguese lady the same evening; and after dark a light was seen to rise from the grave, pass along the cliffs, and seat itself in Madgy's chair at Tol-Pedden. Then, after some hours, it descended, passed back again, and, entering the cottage, rested upon the chest. This curious phenomenon continued for more than three months—nightly—much to the alarm of all but Figgy, who said she knew all about it, and it would be all right in time. One day a strange-looking and strangely attired man arrived at the cottage. Figgy's man (her husband) was at home alone. To him the stranger addressed himself by signs; he could not speak English, so he does not appear to have spoken at all, and expressed a wish to be led to the graves. Away they went, but the foreigner did not appear to require a guide. He at once selected the grave of the lady, and sitting down upon it, he gave vent to his pent-up sorrows. He sent Figgy's man away, and remained there till night, when the light arose from

the grave more brilliant then ever, and proceeded directly to the hut, resting as usual on the chest, which was now covered up with old sails, and all kinds of fishermen's lumber.

The foreigner swept these things aside, and opened the chest. He selected everything belonging to the lady, refusing to take any of the other valuables. He rewarded the wreckers with costly gifts, and left them—no one knowing from whence he came nor whither he went. Madgy Figgy was now truly triumphant. "One witch knows another witch, dead or living," she would say, "and the African would have been the death of us if we hadn't kept the treasure, whereas now we have good gifts, and no gainsaying 'em". Some do say they have seen the light in Madgy Figgy's chair since those times.

***POPULAR ROMANCES OF THE WEST OF ENGLAND*, ROBERT HUNT**

left: ***Witch Raising a Storm*, Leo Bates, early 20th century, American**

In this early 20th-century illustrations, a witch dances on the cliff-edge near her cauldron, to raise a storm to drive a vessel onto the rocks.

The witch's grotto

"Here is my mansion, within the rugged bowels of this cave, This crag, this cliff, this den, which to behold would freeze to ice the hissing trammels of Medusa."

***THE SEVEN CHAMPIONS OF CHRISTENDOM*, JOHN KIRKE**

Nature is traditionally regarded as female. From her womb deep beneath the earth, bountiful Mother Nature brings forth all we need to sustain life: food, shelter, water and warmth. She is the great provider. But she is also the great withholder. If she chooses not to provide, famine, drought and disasters follow, taking away life from those who dwell on her form. Women have always been identified with nature, for their seemingly magical ability to bring forth new life. In growing new generations from bare seed, our bodies might be thought to share in the primal secrets of plants and soil. If this is the case, we must partake in the dualistic nature of Mother Earth, at once kind nurturer and witch, who can choose to hurt by withholding her gifts and causing chaos. We are closer to the Earth than men, but closer also to the underworld beneath the soil. Witches are often depicted inhabiting caverns or grottos, part of the hidden dark womb (or, more frighteningly, the bowels) of the Earth.

right: ***Witch in a Cave*, Salvatore Rosa, 1646, Italian**

This witch has cast a circle, echoed in the circlet of greenery worn around the head, and studies a book of spells, symbol of great learning.

Worshipping Mother Nature

Paganism is thought to be the fastest-growing religion in the world. The word "pagan" encompasses many ways of thinking and ritual practices, but at the heart of this pluralistic nature religion stands the witch. She may refer to herself as a Wiccan, a hedge-witch or solitary, a practitioner of the Craft or devotee of the Goddess. She may join with others on an established path or choose to seek out her own spiritual route map. What remains constant is her devotion to the earth, which is reflected in a life that revolves around the cycle of the seasons and a belief that nature, including our bodies and thoughts, is inherently holy. In her practice, a witch might pay homage to particular places, from mountains and trees to springs and rocks; and on a domestic level tend to the spirit of the hearth or threshold. Homage is paid to the spirit of place with ceremonial acts such as chanting, lighting candles and offering gifts, libation and prayer. This spirit of place might be regarded literally as a guardian divinity. Different divinities, if thought of as female, may be aspects of one great goddess, and if male of one horned god, her consort, whose interaction keeps the Universe in balance (think of the Chinese yin-yang symbol). Others regard various divinities as expressions of a supreme divine principle, a way of approaching the essentially unknowable. However, the female aspect of divinity holds a special place in most pagan belief systems.

Modern witchcraft is not a continuum of worship that can trace its roots back to the past practice of an "old" Mother Goddess religion. It is more creatively vibrant and less dogmatic than this might suggest, honouring individual creativity and the emotional life over the hard facts of academics and historians. This is exemplified by the new names members adopt on committing to the path, and seen in its mythologies and rituals, which are woven from the personal and the emotional alongside sources as diverse as Buddhism, Hinduism, shamanism, feminism, therapeutic practices and the writings of two prominent postwar neo-pagans. The anthropologist Margaret Murray theorized that witchcraft was the remnants of a pre-Christian nature religion or fertility cult persecuted by the church. Occultist Gerald Gardner wrote modern witchcraft's first book (in fictional form), before creatively scripting its rites in the *Book of Shadows*. Though his own work, he claimed to have learned much of its content from his muse, "Old Dorothy", who came from an unbroken line of witches who had passed rites and beliefs down generations of daughters since the 16th century. Other modern witches claim to have inherited rituals and knowledge from family sources, or from local traditions that pre-date Gardner's works. What matters perhaps more than its provenance is the nature of this faith. It is a flexible and innovative form of spirituality that acknowledges what it has borrowed and allows in the chaotic and complex, the intuitive and inconsistent, the feeling-based and the fictitious. One would not expect less of a movement that champions the feminine principle.

"Old Meg she was a Gipsey,
And liv'd upon the Moors;
Her bed it was the brown heath turf,
And her house was out of doors.

Her apples were swart blackberries,
Her currants, pod's o'broom;
Her wine was dew of the wild white rose,
Her book a churchyard tomb.

Her Brothers were the craggy hills,
Her Sisters larchen trees;
Alone with her great family
She liv'd as she did please.

No breakfast had she many a morn,
No dinner many a noon,
And 'stead of supper, she would stare
Full hard against the moon.

But every morn, of woodbine fresh
She made her garlanding,
And, every night, the dark glen Yew
She wove, and she would sing.

And with her fingers, old and brown,
She plaited Mats o' Rushes,
And gave them to the cottagers
She met among the Bushes.

Old Meg was brave as Margaret Queen
And tall as Amazon;
An old red blanket cloak she wore,
A chip hat had she on.
God rest her aged bones somewhere!
She died full long agone!"

***MEG MERRILIES*, JOHN KEATS**

following page: **Detail from *The November Witch*, Artist unknown, early 20th century, American**

The old woman gathers faggots among the birch trees, and her slippers echo the toadstools, suggestive of shamanic flying.

The witch's year

The wheel of the year around which many modern witches order their lives is based on the Celtic calendar. This takes as its inspiration the agricultural year—of sowing seed, germination, harvesting and the quiet darkness of the time when new life is tucked away under the soil. The Celts divided the year in two. On 1 May began the lighted half of the year, or summer, marked with the festival of Beltane. On 1 November celebrated on its eve, Samhaim began the dark half of the year, or winter. In between lie the minor quarter-day festivals: Imbolc (1 Feb), a purification festival marking the return of the light and the first springings of new life; and Lammas (1 August), a celebration of the first harvest. Also celebrated are the cross-quarter days of the summer and winter solstices (Litha in June and Yule in December) and the spring and autumn equinoxes (Ostara for the goddess Eostre in March and Mabon in September). Modern witches might compare the changing seasons to the triple aspects of the Great Goddess, which they will track through the changing Moon each month as well as through the year. At Imbolc, the Goddess appears as a maiden, symbolized by a waxing crescent Moon; at harvest as a mother (the Full Moon), and with each Hallowe'en as a crone (a waning crescent Moon).

Now that most of us live in cities and food comes not out of the earth in its season but is air-freighted around the globe, an agricultural calendar might appeal as a way of keeping us in touch with the turning seasons as much as ensuring that the spokes stay evenly placed around the wheel. However, this calendar does not have to coincide with the Celtic model. While maintaining the two most important calendar events that slice the year in half, many witches are adapting it to reflect their own cultural traditions, from Santeria to Candomble.

Summer is a'come

Beltane (from the Old Irish *beltene*, "bright fire") is celebrated on 1 May and is the second most important festival of the year for followers of the Goddess. At dawn, the May Queen or Flower Bride awakens from her winter slumber and greets the Green Man (represented by a sapling or maypole bedecked with ribbon and greenery). The world rejoices with ribald frolicking worthy of a fertility festival that marks the coming together of the Goddess with her consort. In festivities unbroken in tradition since ancient times and enjoyed by pagans and regular folk alike, greenery plays an obvious role, hauled in after midnight from the wood to dress towns—whole boughs might be tied to lampposts and above doorways and sills, dressed with flowers and ribbons—and a mortal May Queen may be elected to serve for a year.

Great fires play a major role in this festival, for which beacons were once lit atop hills and earthworks, the dwelling place of witches. Leaping the flames or a broomstick seals relationships for the summer to come, and couples might choose to do this as a public way of declaring their relationship. This "handfasting", a joining together or trial marriage, sanctifies the relationship for an agreed length of time—perhaps the time of the festivities, commonly a year and a day, or "for all time", a term used by modern witches to signify life in this world and those beyond; reincarnation is a common belief among modern pagans.

right: **Detail from *May Queen Ceremony*, Photographer unknown, 1923, British**

A girl crowned with flowers, the May Queen. Catholic parishes might crown statues of the Holy Virgin with flowers, for May is considered to be Mary's month.

Winter's witch

The Gaelic witch or goddess of winter and storms is the *Cailleach Bheur* (*bheur* means "sharp"). Her time begins at Hallowe'en. Some tales conflate her with the Hallowe'en hag, who, in the wheel of the Celtic seasons, presides over a quiet but powerful time of darkness, when there is little to do on the land and one might gather around a fire, reflecting, remembering and giving thanks for what has gone and planning what is to come. Hibernating is the best retreat from the angry storms and blizzards associated with the Cailleach. It is said in some parts of Scotland that it is she who raises tempests and whose frosts destroy any impudent shoots of new life that peep through by striking the ground sharply with her stick or wand. This is not the time for new life. She casts a winter-white plaid blanket over the land as she rides abroad, like the Germanic winter goddess Hulda (*aka* Holde, Frau Holle or the White Lady), who, as she shakes out her bedding or cloak makes snow fall on the Earth. Holda may be depicted as a goose (her bedding and cloak are of goosedown), but this Mother Goose can be as cruel as Hans Christian Anderson's Snow Queen, who though "fair and beautiful" is made of ice; "shining and glittering ice". The Cailleach travels aback a wolf. Like huntress goddesses such as Diana and the Lady of the Wild Beast of ancient civilizations, she presides over all wild creatures, including deer and wolves, and if placated will tell deserving hunters which they may take.

left: *Wood Witch*, Florence Harrison, 1912, British

This winter hag resembles the White Lady Frau Holle, who shakes down snow as she flies over northern Europe.

In one legend, the annual washing of the Cailleach's plaid creates the whirlpool of Corryvreckan, or *Coire Bhreacain*, one of the wildest waters off Scotland, much feared by sailors and declared "un-navigable" in parts by Britain's Royal Navy. In other tales, this intense natural maelstrom of treacherous waters is referred to as her cauldron. Its intense currents and high-peaked waves are formed by flood tides hitting a steep pyramid of rock, known as the Hag, and her roaring can be heard 16 km (10 miles) away. The Cailleach is also said to have scattered a number of mountains and lochs across Scotland, Ireland and their Isles by dropping boulders from her apron or basket as she passes over, and she is thought to retreat to one of them when her season of rule ends, with the coming of spring.

"I know you can tie all the winds of the world with a piece of twine. If a sailor unties one knot, he has a fair wind; when he unties the second, it blows hard; but if the third and fourth are loosened, then comes a storm, which will root up whole forests."

***THE SNOW QUEEN*, HANS CHRISTIAN ANDERSEN**

The Thunder Hag

One day in midsummer, when all the land was bathed in warm, bright sunshine and the sea was lulled to sleep, the Thunder Hag came over Scotland in a black chariot drawn by fierce red hounds and surrounded by heavy clouds. The sky was darkened, and as the hag drew near, the rattling of the chariot wheels and the baying of the hounds sounded loud and fearsome. She rode from sea to sea, over hill and moor, and threw fireballs at the deep forests, which set them ablaze. Terror spread through the land as the chariot passed in smoke and clouds.

On the next day the hag came back. She threw more fireballs on forests of fir and silver birch, and they burned fiercely. Dry heather on the moors and the sun-dried grass were also swept by flame.

The king was greatly troubled, and he sent forth his chief warriors to slay the hag; but they fled in terror when they saw her coming near.

***WONDER TALES FROM SCOTTISH MYTH AND LEGEND*,**

DONALD ALEXANDER MACKENZIE

Raging Earth goddesses

"So there with angry hands she broke the ploughs
That turned the soil and sent to death alike
The farmer and his labouring ox, and bade
The fields betray their trust, and spoilt the seeds.
False lay the island's famed fertility,
Famous through all the world. The young crops died
In the first blade, destroyed now by the rain
Too violent, now by the sun too strong.
The stars and winds assailed them; hungry birds
Gobbled the scattered seeds; thistles and twitch,
Unconquerable twitch, wore down the wheat."

***METAMORPHOSES*, OVID**

Nature goddesses spend some months on the Earth, bringing fruitfulness and warmth, and then retreat from us. In Greek mythology, she is Demeter, queen of grain, crops and bountiful harvest, and patron of those who till the soil (she still is; the Demeter mark certifies that produce has been farmed biodynamically, sown and harvested to the phases of the moon). But one day, Demeter's daughter Persephone was abducted by the god of the underworld, Hades. Lured by a "toy", a marvellous fake flower, she is seized by Hades, who bears her away in his "golden car". Only Hecate, queen of the underworld, hears the girl "loudly crying" to her father and mother as the god carries her away in his chariot "down to his realm of mist and gloom". In search of Persephone, the stricken Demeter rages around the world looking, hour by hour from sunrise to sunset and on through the night, unable to do anything else: not speak, eat, drink nor wash. Some accounts have it that despite her stricken state, the lustful god Poseidon pursues her. She turns herself into a mare to flee his advances, but he becomes a stallion and rapes her. (She later gives birth to the monstrous snake-headed Medusa).

Beyond her senses, Demeter disfigures her form, becoming an old woman, puts on black clothing and retreats to a cave. By becoming the archetypal witch and withholding her bounty, she brings mankind near starvation, as nature stands still and crops fail. Finally, the great god Zeus forces Persephone's rescue "that her mother may see her with her eyes and cease from her dread anger". With this, Demeter returns from her self-imposed exile, making the word fruitful once more, but during her time in the underworld Persephone has eaten pomegranate seeds, and must return to that dark, cold place for four months of the year; Demeter withholds her gifts each year when her daughter is taken from her anew. Mother Nature is as cruel as she is bountiful.

Into the woods

The traditional dwelling place of witches, the forest, represents the dangers waiting to assault those who venture beyond the boundaries of civilization and conventional norms. Many women accused of witchcraft claim to have first encountered the devil or his demonic messengers at the edge of the forest, and the setting of the film *The Blair Witch Project* (1999) shows that they lurk here still, and that deep in the woods, the horror is all the more intense for happening "off-screen".

The forest is an especially rich motif in Germanic folk tales, not surprisingly, since much of Germany was forested when the Grimms were collecting their stories (one quarter is wooded still). In their work, the forest is a place where the natural and supernatural worlds touch the world we know. The psychologist Carl Jung identified the forest with the unconscious and with the feminine principle, suggesting that the dark branches of its vast canopy shield those within its realm from the masculine, solar power of reason. In Russian lore, the capricious, "feminine" quality of the forest is embodied in the *lesh'yi*, a shape-shifting creature associated with death who toys with those who enter her domain. She can choose to trick them with shape and sound: echoes, sweet breezes, rustling leaves, the brushing of twig fingers or shadows glimpsed in the next glade draw the innocent more deeply into her lair. But if she is given due respect, the *lesh'yi* may reward mortals with her riches. While the forest is a place of danger and the uncanny, it is also a place of bounty: only by venturing beyond the limits of the civilized world can we hunt, forage and find water. The forest is also a source of comfort: its wood provides fuel, its moss and leaves the filling for a mattress. In fairy tales, woods often offer sanctuary to those fleeing witch figures. In the forest, Snow White and Hansel and Gretel find relief (at first) from the terrifying desires of their wicked stepmothers. By losing their way in the forest, they also lose their old selves and gain new reserves of self-confidence and self-reliance that might equip them to outwit future witches. The forest is a place of magical transformation and those who pass its exacting tests will change and thrive. In the Hindu tradition, the forest is not only a place of supernatural happenings but of spiritual transformation. We are urged to retreat there during the final phase of life in order to renounce the material world, explore the spirit and journey towards enlightenment and the world beyond.

following page: ***Hansel and Gretel in the Forest*, Charles Robinson, early 20th century, British**

Lost in the dark woods, Hansel and Gretel cling together as the roots of the trees threaten to trap the children by binding their limbs fast.

"There was once an old castle in the midst of a large and thick forest, and in it an old woman who was a witch dwelt all alone. In the daytime she changed herself into a cat or a screech-owl, but in the evening she took her proper shape again as a human being. She could lure wild beasts and birds to her, and then she killed and boiled and roasted them. If anyone came within one hundred paces of the castle he was obliged to stand still, and could not stir from the place until she bade him be free. But whenever an innocent maiden came within this circle, she changed her into a bird, and shut her up in a wickerwork cage, and carried the cage into a room in the castle. She had about seven thousand cages of rare birds in the castle."

"JORINDE AND JORINGEL", IN *HOUSEHOLD TALES*, JACOB AND WILHELM GRIMM, TRANS. MARGARET HUNT

House of Horror

Interview with Eduardo Sánchez

Cuban-born Eduardo Sánchez is co-writer, co-director and co-editor (with Dan Myrick) of the cult classic horror film *The Blair Witch Project* (1999), one of the most profitable movies in motion-picture history (from budget to gross), which introduced the world to the best-known movie witch of modern times, Elly Kedward. With his blairwitch.com website, Eduardo created an innovative and highly influential form of web-marketing. He is co-founder of Haxan Films and an award-winning director of commercials.

Why did you choose to create a horror film around a witch, rather than, say, a werewolf or a beast?

Dan and I felt that the evil presence in the woods had to have a supernatural element, but be rooted in a real person. We did consider a male figure, but that seemed to make the film too "Merlinesque", so we based the film around a witch legend we made up dating from the late 1700s, a while after the Salem craze. It seemed to make sense in a small town setting. Our Blair Witch—her name is Elly Kedward, though you have to pay close attention to hear her name in the film—was a medicine woman who could heal people, deliver babies and deal in herbs, but she wasn't a very conventional person and was eventually ostracized and condemned to death. It's a tragic tale really.

Did you draw on your Cuban heritage in creating her?

Yes, this was very influential. Mom raised us Catholic and I was born in rural Cuba in a community where there was very little education and people had a fear of *santería*, a Cuban version of voodoo rooted in an African tradition. Here, witches were mostly women and you weren't supposed to mess with them. Mom told tales of a *santera*, or witch, near town who everyone else shunned, and then their crops would fall or bad stuff would happen. So I learned that you don't fool about with witches.

The witch never appears in the movie. Indeed, it was you, the production team, who played her role off-screen, terorizing the actors every night. How did that feel?

We didn't know how it would work. We had to use the limited resources we had. We toyed with the idea of showing the witch as an older woman covered with horse fur, and with special effects—like ending the film with a levitating witch and great fireworks—only we had no budget.

How much did the actors know about what the witch would do to them?

Not much. We gave away a bit at the auditions, but we kept as much of the plot to ourselves as possible. Mike Williams still tells how freaked out he was to be woken in the night by a bunch of kids laughing outside the tent.

So you really were like a witch; having knowledge of the future, but choosing to withhold it?

Yes, we were toying with them. And we did have fun doing it. We controlled those actors' lives for seven or eight days. We woke them at night, and when the food ran out, we kept their rations low. So real exhaustion set in. Being lost in the woods, hungry, tired and with no modern conveniences (we took away their cell phones), they had to tap into their inner spirit, their primal ancestry. We don't do that too much in modern society; we tend to shun religion and everything that can't be explained. And it got pretty deep; there were scenes we had to cut when Mike lost it completely—he was pounding trees, crying, rocking himself....

What sources were you drawing on when you chose to set the witch and her house of horror deep in the woods?

Dan and I grew up with the Grimm's tales, which, to me, stem from scary stories told around the campfire at the end of the day. For me, to be lost in the woods is one of the most scary of experiences—to this day I find camping fearful! In modern-day America. There are few places you can go that are exactly the way they were thousands of years ago, but the forest is a place you can cut out civilization completely and be really isolated. Feel what it was like to be one of the early humans. And with our budget, it was the only option.

Though she doesn't appear in the film, the witch Elly Kedward seems to have taken on a life of her own.

Yes, she's definitely taken off. A bunch of people on MySpace are obsessed by her, and there's a website, too, *The Trial of Elly Kedward*. Dan and I have talked about making a movie of her life—in fact, whenever we mention it, it gets more press than anything else we say. But we don't own the idea any more. Just like with the witches in *The Crucible*, people seem to feel an emotional tie to Elly's story, and the misunderstanding and injustice meted out to her. History repeats itself: *The Crucible* reflected anxiety about a red scare; this witch maybe reflects our anxiety about terrorism and how fear of terrorism manipulates us to the same tragic endings.

The Wood Witch

A king was once hunting in a great wood, and he hunted the game so eagerly that none of his courtiers could follow him. When evening came on he stood still and looked round him, and he saw that he had quite lost himself. He sought a way out, but could find none. Then he saw an old woman with a shaking head coming towards him; but she was a witch.

"Good woman," he said to her, "can you not show me the way out of the wood?"

"Oh, certainly, Sir King," she replied, "I can quite well do that, but on one condition, which if you do not fulfil you will never get out of the wood, and will die of hunger."

"What is the condition?" asked the king.

"I have a daughter," said the old woman, "who is so beautiful that she has not her equal in the world, and is well fitted to be your wife; if you will make her lady-queen I will show you the way out of the wood."

The king in his anguish of mind consented, and the old woman led him to her little house where her daughter was sitting by the fire. She received the king as if she were expecting him, and he saw that she was certainly very beautiful; but she did not please him, and he could not look at her without a secret feeling of horror. As soon as he had lifted the maiden on to his horse the old woman showed him the way, and the king reached his palace, where the wedding was celebrated.

The king had already been married once, and had by his first wife seven children, six boys and one girl, whom he loved more than anything in the world. And now, because he was afraid that their stepmother might not treat them well and might do them harm, he put them in a lonely castle that stood in the middle of a wood. It lay so hidden, and the way to it was so hard to find, that he himself could not have found it out had not a wise-woman given him a reel of thread which possessed a marvellous property: when he threw it before him it unwound itself and showed him the way. But the king went so often to his dear children that the Queen was offended at his absence. She grew curious, and wanted to know what he had to do quite alone in the wood. She gave his servants a great deal of money, and they betrayed the secret to her, and also told her of the reel which alone could point out the way. She had no rest now till she had found out where the king guarded the reel, and then she made some little white shirts and, as she had learnt from her witch-mother, sewed an enchantment in each of them.

And when the king had ridden off she took the little shirts and went into the wood, and the reel showed her the way. The children, who saw someone coming in the distance, thought it was their dear father coming to them, and sprang to meet him very joyfully. Then she threw over each one a little shirt, which when it had touched their bodies changed them into swans and they flew away over the forest.

"THE SIX SWANS", IN *THE YELLOW FAIRY BOOK,* THE BROTHERS GRIMM

ED. ANDREW LANG

following page: ***The Six Swans*, H.J. Ford, early 20th century, British**

The witch's daughter changes her stepchildren into swans with enchantments sewn into their shirts.

The Six Brothers Changed Into Swans by Their Stepmother.

“Now Pitcher the Witch, being mad with shame and spite, fled from the face of man, and ran through the woods like a wild wolf. And so she came to Bar Harbor (Pes’sonkqu’), and sat down on a log and said, with her heart full of bitterness and malice, ‘I would that I could become something which should torment all men.’ And as she said this she became a mosquito (T'sis-o), and so it came to pass that mosquitoes were made.”

THE ALGONQUIN LEGENDS OF NEW ENGLAND,

CHARLES G. LELAND (1884)

The witch wood

"The witches in Slavonian gypsy-lore have now and then parties which meet to spin, always by full moonlight on a cross-road. But it is not advisable…to pass by on such occasions, as the least they do to the heedless wayfarer is to bewitch and sink him into a deep sleep. But they are particularly fond of assembling socially in the tops of trees, especially of the ash, walnut, and linden or lime kinds, preferring those whose branches grow in the manner here depicted [a trident shape]."

***GYPSY SORCERY AND FORTUNE-TELLING*, CHARLES GODFREY LELAND**

The mountain ash, or rowan, is known as the "witch tree" or "Lady of the Mountain", and was the tree in Norse lore from which the first woman was created. It is a sign of vibrant life in the midst of death; another of its names is the "quicken", for it thrives even on poor soils and at heights where little else will grow. It is strongly associated with witches; even the dye the tree gives is black. Being the strongest deterrent to witches in the Northern Hemisphere, this is the tree traditionally planted outside the doors of houses and the entrances of homesteads and burial grounds to protect them from witchcraft. In Scandinavia if it roots itself in a seemingly inhospitable place, such as a crevice of rock, the tree is considered even more protective. Boughs might be cut to affix over stables, window and door lintels (and even box beds) for protection on nights of the year when witches were known to be abroad; Walpurgis Night was one. To protect a body from being "fore-spoken", greenwood wands would be folded or broken (never cut with a knife) into charms for the pocket or to sew inside a seam. They might include an equal-armed cross secured with talismanic red thread; charms or sprigs of rowan might also be tied to a cow's horns to protect its milk.

The berries of the rowan are ruby-red, and stand out against the winter landscape, the time of year when the Crone is at the apex of her powers. They may add to this tree's talismanic powers, for red is the most protective of colours against enchantment, confronting the forces of darkness with a symbol of mortal life force, our blood and the blazing sun of dawn after a long winter's night. And deep within each of the berries is hidden a five-pointed star, or pentagram, ancient symbol of the Goddess and of protection.

"Black-luggie, lammer [amber] bead,
Rowan-tree and red thread,
Put the witches to their speed."

SCOTTISH COUNTER-MAGIC CHARM

The nut lady

"To keep children from picking unripe hazelnuts in the Canton of Saint Gall they cry to them, '*S' Haselnussfràuli chumt* The hazelnut lady is coming!'"

***GYPSY SORCERY AND FORTUNE-TELLING*, CHARLES GODFREY LELAND**

The hazel tree and her nuts are allied with wise women and witches across northern Europe and the Celtic world. In German-speaking nations, the bush may be spoken of in passing as *Haselnussfrau*, Lady Hazel, and with some reverence in honour of her powers of regeneration. Even if cut down in the autumn, she returns next spring strengthened and with a greater number of stems. Her leaves are also the first to appear in northern climes and the last to drop, which reflects her prowess in the natural world.

Hazel branches are extremely pliable—they bend easily into shape without breaking and have been put to use in weaving baskets, hedges and the walls of homesteads and animal pens. The wands are useful in charm-making, too, bent into circlets or crosses and adorned with amuletic charms, such as red thread or protective herbs. Being able to "bend" nature is the stuff of witches; indeed, the word "witch" may be related to the Middle English word of Scandinavian origin *wicker*, meaning a small, pliable branch. The word is also used of the willow, a tree associated with the Greek lunar goddess, Hecate, whose devotees used wands of willow stems in their rites.

The native North American healing tree known as "witch hazel" —famed for the astringent, anti-inflammatory and blood-stopping properties of its leaves and bark—is a different species, named because its leaves and habit resemble those of the hazel proper. Its name may also have come about because its clusters of distinctive golden flowers bloom around Hallowe'en, the festival with which it has become associated. It plays up to its witchy image with its long, forked branches like gnarled witch's fingers and a habit of "spitting" out seeds with an audible pop.

Nutting season was a time of year that called for protection—it required innocents to venture into the forest, where devilish strangers lurk (look out for a tell-tale hoof). In Celtic lore, hazelnuts represent higher wisdom—a secret, concentrated form of ever-growing knowledge (the Gaelic word for nut, *cno*, resembles the word for wisdom, *cnocach*). A naturally grown double nut is especially prized. Irish legend tells of nine hazel trees branching over a sacred pool, dropping their nuts of wisdom into the spring. As they fell, they were eaten by magical salmon and showed as bright spots on their flesh. Thus salmon became renowned as the wisest of creatures. There is a tale that the legendary Irish leader Fionn MacCumhill gained his wisdom and shape-shifting powers when splattered with the cooking juice of one of these salmon of knowledge. Those powers might include foresight. Hazelnuts are much used in divination rituals at Hallowe'en.

Wands and dowsing

The all-revealing rod or wand used for divining as well as spell-making is often donated by a tree associated with the witch's powers; in Italy it is a forked branch of hazel, which may have a white metallic sheen or be naturally tinged crimson or purple. In the Celtic world and northern Europe, branches of the rowan tree, willow or apple are used for divining rods. When using a wand, the witch draws in the powers of the elements: earth and water that nourish a tree, air that it breathes in and purifies, and the fire of the sun. She also aligns herself with the powers of life dormant in a winter tree that renew themselves each spring. She concentrates these natural forces at the tip of the wand; this point of intensity equips her to bring about a "little spring" with each magical wave.

Dowsing using a Y-shaped branch to detect something hidden, usually beneath the ground, is an ancient art that seems to be depicted in North African cave paintings some 8,000 years old. Certainly it was being used in Germany by the beginning of the 15th century to detect underground mineral deposits, such as coal, and was denounced, like "water-witching", by Martin Luther as the devil's work. Later, it was used to find lost treasure, animals and even people. In modern times, dowsers have been called in by the US marines and multinational energy companies to clear mines and find oil. Research at Munich University found dowsers more successful at predicting potable water sources than geohydrologists. Hazel is reputedly the best material for dowsing for water and rowan for metal ores; witch hazel is used to detect water, salt and precious metals.

Edmund
Dulac

Mandrake

**"I last night lay all alone
O' the ground, to hear the mandrake groan;
And pluck'd him up, though he grew full low:
And, as I had done, the cock did crow."**

***THE MASQUE OF QUEENS*, BEN JONSON (1609)**

A native of the Mediterranean region, the narcotic root mandrake is the plant most often associated with witches and their deadly potions; other names for it include Herb of Circe, Satan's Apple and Witch's Manikin. The mandrake takes its magical charge as much from its appearance as its medicinal properties: the "man-dragon fiend" resembles a tiny human figure with gnarled limbs. Both sexes are on offer—the male is phallus-like, the female forked at the legs, and a couple may be entwined in fantastical sexual positions. The first and last especially were used in fertility and aphrodisiac potions, and have been carried as love and child-wishing charms since ancient Egyptian times. They could be placed under a pillow to bring dreams or consulted in divination rituals (some were said to talk, nod or shake hands to tell of their predictions). Other uses for the mandrake include as a poppet-type pin-figure, or in "flying ointment", for the root has hallucinogenic and narcotic properties.

The deadly charge of this plant (it can kill) is reflected in the lore attached to it. It was reputed to scream and sweat blood when uprooted, and all who heard the cry were said to perish. For this reason, it was thought to be harvested by trained dogs at night, and with much magic ceremony. The mandrake root was thought to grow beneath gallows trees, propagated from the body fluids of unrepentant murderers or the unbapitzed, and in some regions merely to own one was proof of being a witch. Witches in 17th-century France and Germany have been executed on this evidence. Still today a mandrake root commands great respect and ceremony. It may be kept in a specially crafted wooden case (some are shaped like a miniature coffin) or be wrapped in crimson silk, especially if employed for love magic; the roots are nurtured and, some say, even fed and watered with wine. When concocted with care by adepts, potions made from this plant of the gods (now a controlled substance in many countries) are said to induce a state of euphoria that introduces the user to her own inner wisdom.

previous page: ***And Her Godmother Pointed to the Finest of all her Wands*, Edmund Dulac, 1910, French**

Cinderella's fairy godmother has only to direct the tip of her wand at a pumpkin to transform it into a coach fit for a princess.

following page: ***The Witch and the Mandrake*, Henry Fuseli, 19th century, Swiss**

Taking this toxic plant causes the pupils to dilate and the eyes to stop producing tears, both defining signs of a witch. Its name was synonymous in Italy with the enchantress Circe, who transformed wild animals into narcotic day-dreamers and turned men to swine with her herbal potions.

“There was an old woman tost up in a blanket,
Seventeen times as high as the moon,
What she did there, no mortal can tell,
But under her arm she carried a broom.
Old woman, old woman, old woman, said I,
O whither, O whither, O whither so high?
To sweep the cobwebs from the sky,
And I shall be back again by and by.”

MOTHER GOOSE RHYME

right: ***Old Mother Goose*, Frederick Richardson, 1915, British**

Some witches don’t fly on broomsticks—they are intertwined in lore with birds. One such is *Mother Goose* with witch’s hat, cape and broom flying over a winter landscape, like the northern European winter goddess Mother Holle, on a white goose.

Old Mother Goose, when
She wanted to wander,
Would ride through the air
On a very fine gander.

Airbourne antics

Though associated with the earthly domain and its plants, the sea and storms, witches have great affinity with the air; "...they made themselves air", writes Macbeth to his wife, to explain how his three witches vanished, frustrating his desire to question them further about his future. The classical writer Festus names a *lamiaa*, or witch, as Volatica—she who flies. In flying more than any other magical act, the witch flaunts her ability to transcend the principles of time and space, and the mores of the world below. She shows how free she is to move upwards and onwards between worlds, from whence she accesses powers such as prophecy. By defying the laws of gravity, the human body and danger (physical and psychic), the witch defies the stereotype of the weak female—and seems to revel in the performance, like a death-defying circus flyer. Perhaps this is why, despite all the bad publicity, we remain attracted to this thrill-seeker. During World War II, the fear engendered in Germany by Soviet woman fighter pilots engaged in daring low-level bombing was so intense that they were nicknamed the "night witches". When she flies through the skies, the witch is no longer Eve, the fallen woman, but claims a space with the angels.

The earliest depiction of a witch riding a broom, her most popular modern vehicle, is thought to be carved in Schleswig Cathedral in Germany, and dates from around 1280. Generally at this time, witches were shown riding goats—the creature most often associated with Satan. Sometimes they rode backward, as if to emphasize their threat to the general order. Early modern theologians suggested that the witch could not fly by her own volition, but required diabolical help.

The Gospels of Sts. Matthew and Luke describe the devil transporting Jesus to the tops of temples and mountains, so one might infer that it would be no feat to carry mere women.

Not until the late 15th century does the goat become transformed into a broomstick in central and northern Europe, an item that emphasizes the homely nature of witches. No longer demonically powered sorceresses or harpy-like birds, witches need only a humble, everyday cleaning implement to do their worst. With such a potent sign of witchcraft in every home, anyone could be accused of witchcraft. Not for nothing in Sicily do they refer to witches as *patruni di casa*, mistresses of the house. In Tanzania in 2003, a regional police commander told the BBC that any aged old lady with red eyes was believed to be a witch: red eyes are a result of cooking over a smoky fire for decades. In other cultures and eras, the witch rides other domestic implements: Baba Yaga, Russia's grandmother hag, steers her way across the sky in a great iron mortar, stirring her way through the currents with its pestle (she covers her tracks by sweeping away the trail with a kitchen broom). African witches travel in sieves, like their early modern European counterparts. Some witches are even shown on early "surfboards". The Witch of Newbury (executed in 1763) was spotted by a bunch of astounded soldiers performing tricks on a board on a river: "to and fro she fleeted on the board standing firm bolt upright…turning and winding it which way she pleased, making it pastime to her…".

Some commentators relate a witch's flying to the skills of the shaman, who goes on an ecstatic spiritual flight. By inducing a trance, he negates his body and liberates his soul to commune with the forces of nature. The altered state is achieved through drums and

dancing, by careful and learned use of natural hallucinogens, and by putting on a mask or feathered cloak that aligns his spirit with the higher intelligence of totemic animals or birds. From his state of heightened awareness, he absorbs wisdom to bring back to the community. One of the most popular recipes for flying ointment, with which witches were reputed to anoint themselves in order to fly (or achieve an ecstatic state) was said to be concocted from a blend of highly toxic psychoactive plants, namely the poisons hemlock, deadly nightshade (or belladonna) and wolfsbane (or aconite). In minute quantities, they can cause euphoria and delirium; in not much larger quantities, death. Hemlock has a sedative and analgesic action (in large doses it can cause paralysis); narcotic deadly nightshade anesthetizes, relaxes the muscles and nervous system and dilates the pupils; while the poison wolfsbane works on the heart and nervous system. Such a heady mix might indeed produce an out-of-body experience. Someone who regularly undertakes such experiences might achieve spiritual enlightenment or the ability to learn from different states of consciousness, such as dreaming. This is the witch's true lightness of being.

previous page: ***Witch Flies on a Broom*, artist unknown, date unknown, British**

This witch doesn't need to be seated on her broom shaft nor use it in the most aerodynamic way to take to the air. Here, she carries it in her hands as a spindle.

The Best Brooms

In any case, it is not the material used to make the broom which makes a lot of difference in the flying technique, but how often it has been used to sweep the house: the best flying brooms are those which have often been held by expert hands for housecleaning tasks. Many tests have been carried out to prove the point: a holly broom made for the shed floor usually flies nicely. One can even use a bundle of sloe branches, as long as it has been used two or three times to sweep the hearth. Not that it flies quickly or that it is comfortable to sit on, on account of the thorns, not to mention the resulting rips in the skirt. But it does fly, like any other broom, if it is put in the hands of a woman old enough to be experienced in the art of sweeping.

***WALPURGISNACHT*, YANN GERVEN**

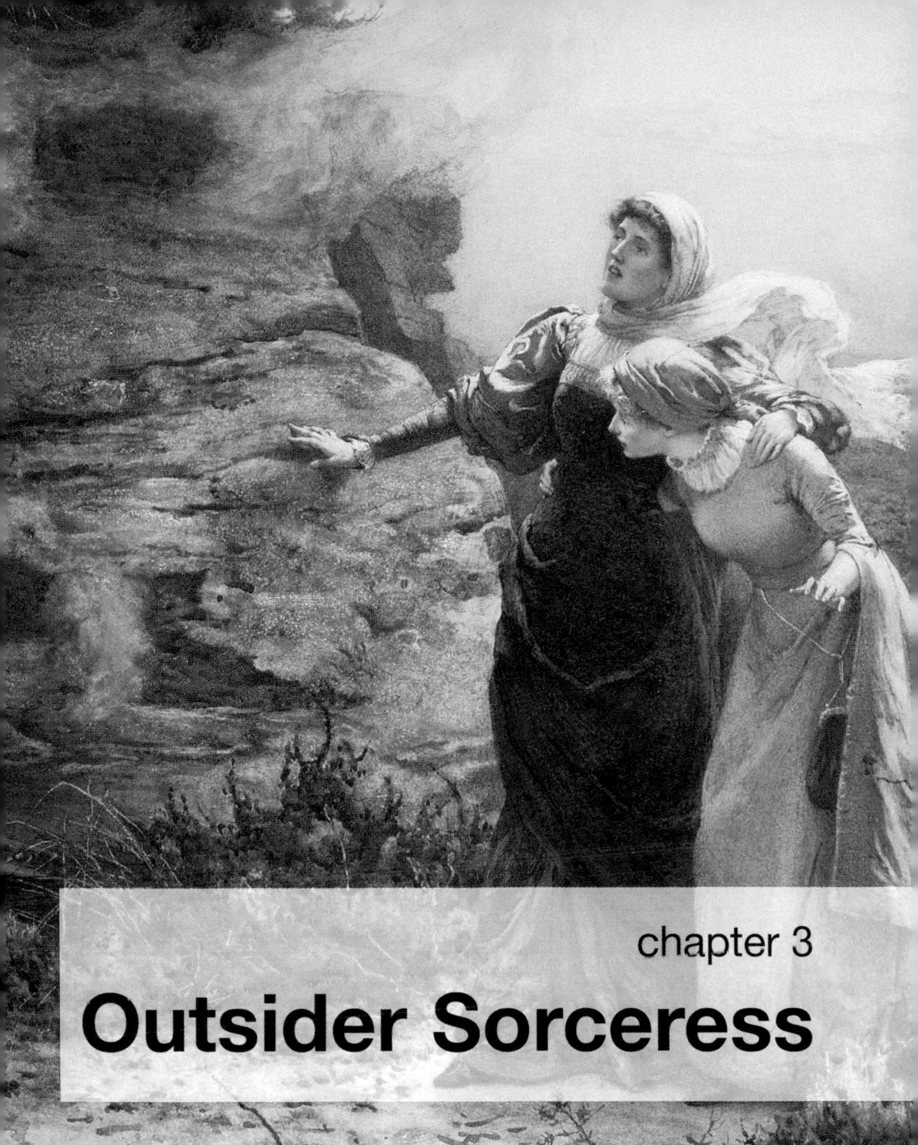

chapter 3

Outsider Sorceress

The ladies from outside

**"Remote from sheltered village green,
On a hill's northern side she dwelt,
Where from sea-blasts the hawthorns lean,
And hoary dews are slow to melt."**

***GOODY BLAKE AND HARRY GILL*, *A TRUE STORY*,**
WILLIAM WORDSWORTH

In Sicily one doesn't refer to witches by name. That would incur their wrath or draw their interest. One refers to them as *donna di fuori*, "ladies from outside". Throughout the world, witches are kept behind boundaries, safely held at arm's length from the day-to-day life of a community. The witch leads a solitary existence on a mountain-top,

previous page: ***A Visit to the Witch*, Edward Frederick Brewtnall, 19th century, British**
Living on the outskirts—in the wilderness—is an initiatory test in many cultures for those who wish to follow a shamanic path or devote time to the spiritual life.

right: ***The Arrest*, Artist unknown, 19th century, American**
An elderly woman is lead away by an officer of the law during the time of the Salem witch trials. Accused by her community, she holds out her hands in a gesture of innocence.

MASTER·
Hopewell Pegge
Ye
Tallowe Chandler
H·P.

just beyond the village limits or deep within a wood, where the ordered life of the community blurs into unpredictability and wildness. Indeed, the word "hag" may derive from the Old English word *haga*, meaning "hedge" or "boundary". Some lived literally on the edge of the known world: the classical witches Circe and Medea inhabited islands and foreign lands far removed geographically from the civilized world of ancient Greece—and morally, for theirs were places defined by sensual pleasures, indolence, rage and insanity. Their weird sister Hecate inhabits a psychically distant place, the underworld, a liminal zone between this world and unknown futures. Sinful Eve and wicked Pandora demonstrate the need to keep the two worlds separate when they choose to venture off alone to meet the serpent-tempter or open the box of hellish delights.

"But where is he to find the Witch-maiden?" said the first bird. "She has no settled dwelling, but is here to-day and gone to-morrow. He might as well try to catch the wind."

***THE DRAGON OF THE NORTH* IN *THE YELLOW FAIRY BOOK*,**
ED. ANDREW LANG

In fairy tales the places that witches inhabit are often markedly different from regular homes. In Hans Christian Anderson's *The Snow Queen* (which contains not one but five witch figures), the first witch that Gerda meets on her quest to find Kay lives in a place of perpetual spring. Hansel and Gretel's witch's home is made of bread, in later tellings iced and decorated gingerbread. Baba Yaga's home is equally deadly, but more obviously decorated: a hut on chicken legs adorned with row upon row of human bones capped with skulls whose eyes glitter so brightly that the coal-black night becomes as light as day.

Maintaining boundaries helps to make society seem ordered. If everything you can control is neatly categorized and contained (and everything you can't nicely defined and excluded), it's more likely that that chaos, which threatens a tidy, ordered, bright existence, can be kept at the door and structures and hierarchies keep running as they always have. This might seem especially important at times of extremis, such as the climate-change years known as the Little Ice Age from 1560 to the mid 17th century, when revolts, famine and economic crisis ravaged Europe and accusations of witchcraft peaked. During this era, keeping up the boundaries was women's work suggests the historian Diane Purkiss. The good wife kept her realm clean and well-ordered, making good use of all the raw materials that crossed her threshold, from milk to flax to seasonal herbs. Using practical, everyday magic she churned milk into butter and cheese, boiled fresh fruit into life-suspending preserves, spun, wove, stitched and mended clothes, and brewed herbal remedies. With such care, the housewife kept outsider elements at bay, those opportunistic wild cards that threatened her precarious domestic life, such as wool mites, viruses, mold and wear and tear. Human life was precarious before refrigeration, central heating, antibiotics and a year-round supply of food and clothing. Any let-up in housewifely vigilance—should she ride her broom, not sweep with it, for example—could bring the whole edifice tumbling down. Therefore the good wife learned to become extra vigilant about items of unknown or suspect provenance entering her home: once boundaries were breached, the nameless ills that belonged to the wild place beyond could enter. A borrowed crock or donated foodstuff might harbour a germ; visitors might have unclean intentions, especially those who lived outside the village or its social structure. Especially those who, despite their social dislocation, were depended upon for their healing potions, ability to find lost objects or administer to women in childbirth. If one such should enter the home and a child fall ill or the milk curdle, the explanation and remedy might lie with the lady from outside. Thus the witch was cast in the role of bad-wife, the housewife's alter ego and the dark shadow she must strive to avoid becoming.

Bewitched!

In the popular American TV series that ran from 1964 to 1972, the protagonist Samantha Stephens struggles to fulfil her role as the perfect all-American housewife. She sincerely wants to get everything right and please her junior ad-exec husband Darrin. The hitch is she's not the girl next door you might expect from her looks, but a witch, and so, by nature, a refusenik when it comes to domestic matters. She determines to try hard to be like other wives, embracing domesticity over sorcery, and doesn't usually conjure up meals or wash pots by magic; she uses real housewifely skills (though she can operate the vacuum with the twitch of her nose). But where's the fun in that? No matter how hard she tries—she agreed after their wedding to keep her magic powers under wraps—she just can't keep her bad-girl genes safely beneath her apron. (Her husband is keen to keep her identity concealed in order to climb the corporate ladder). We cheer as she wrinkles her nose (her magic trick) to wreak havoc with the established order: using her transformative powers, she turns Darrin's boss into a poodle, her husband into a old woman and creates fake Samanthas, each week almost exposing herself and showing up poor Darrin. However, at the end of each episode she chooses to use her powers to restore the established order, safely containing her disruptive influence. We know she can run rings round her husband, but in the end chooses not to. This makes her all the more powerful: Samantha not only has the outsider's magic touch, but the strength of will to choose when to use it.

The Witch's Dilemma

In this scene from the episode of *Bewitched* entitled "Sam in the Moon", Samantha the witch is in a quandary. Should she use enchantment to achieve domestic bliss—and so win time to spend with her hubby—or should she just buckle down like the domestic goddess she pledged to become on her wedding day and use the vacuum? Her mother Endora can't understand how she raised such a moral creature, and pronounces her a "fallen woman".

SAMANTHA: *Vacuum cleaner, I've got a problem. I can spend four hours pushing you around and cleaning out the attic, in which case I won't have any time to spend with Darrin...or....I can....*

(shrugs meaningfully)

you know ... get it all done in a flash and relax for the rest of the afternoon with my husband. What do you think? Should I or shouldn't I....

(She wiggles her nose. The vacuum cleaner goes on and begins to travel rapidly over the rug.)

right: **Ellzabeth Montgomery as Samantha from *Bewitched*, 1965, American**

Elizabeth Montgomery played the witch Samantha in the popular TV series for some years; in this image from January 1965, she holds her familiar Ling-Ling.

Boundary charms

"A rich woman sat up late one night carding and preparing wool while all the family and servants were asleep. Suddenly a knock was given at the door, and a voice called, 'Open! open!'.

'Who is there?' said the woman of the house.

'I am the Witch of the One Horn,' was answered.

The mistress, supposing that one of her neighbours had called and required assistance, opened the door, and a woman entered, having in her hand a pair of wool carders, and bearing a horn on her forehead, as if growing there. She sat down by the fire in silence, and began to card the wool with violent haste."

***ANCIENT LEGENDS, MYSTIC CHARMS AND SUPERSTITIONS OF IRELAND*, LADY FRANCESCA SPERANZA WILDE**

Bewitching often takes place on a property's boundaries: at the doorway or perimeter fence, which is neither in nor out, and around the hearth. Accessible through the chimney, the hearth is the source of food and heat and so a potent symbol of a healthy, happy home. If evil strikes here, it goes straight to the heart. Places of rest are also boundary points—the boundary between the conscious and unconscious world.

Charms were traditionally placed at these points of easy ingress. Windows and the apex of the roof were also protected, the latter a place witches might alight to take a breather during a broomstick ride. Counter-magic charms include branches from trees with protective properties and metal amulets such as horseshoes, an old knife or needle—all over the globe the supernatural world detests iron and steel, bronze, brass and silver. A poker might be placed to rest against the chimney breast or a hearth cloth nailed to the mantelpiece, embroidered with protective symbols, such as stars and zig-zag designs in amuletic red thread. These might be adorned with pompoms, tassels and lace. Knots are witches' work, but also may confuse them, for they are transfixed by labyrinthine structures and complex patterning. Polished or reflective surfaces reflect evil back at its owner, and witch balls blown from hollow green or blue glass have been placed or hung in cottage windows since the 18th century to keep watch over a home, and its family and they were passed down the generations. Some resemble fishermen's floats and in seafaring regions have absorbed some of the lore of sea and weather witches (such as that the evil eye cannot penetrate water). Others might more resemble yuletide baubles, lined with silver the better to reflect harmful thoughts and deeds.

Anti-witch measures were a peculiarly common form of home-insurance until recent years. Many come to light when householders pull out doorsteps or hearth stones, replace windows or disrupt old boundary walls, take up floorboards or repair staircases. In the chimney, they might be perched on a ledge or cached in a deliberably fashioned hideaway, or "spirit midden". The cache of deliberately concealed objects often contains sharp and metallic (for doubly deterrent properties) nails and pins, knives and files. Hand-stitched items, buttons or worn clothing, or garment patterns, particularly children's garments, are often found, but single shoes are the most commonly discovered object. In the UK, the Northampton Museum curates these finds, and usually receives one newly uncovered shoe a month. They come from all periods in history, but are usually well worn and belong to a child. Like horseshoes, they resemble the good-luck charms given to brides for safety and fertility, or perhaps they represent a DNA lure for witches: a footprint is not unlike a fingerprint (and a dress pattern not unlike a body), and witches are particularly attracted to youthful bodies. The shoe might tempt her into a tight space from which she cannot escape.

Witch bottles are a more powerful form of spiritual protection concealed within the fabric of a home, which may be intended to undo a spell or punish the doer of suspected witchery. They comprise a brew of the victim's DNA—her urine, hair or nail clippings—and healing herbs, salt or organ-shaped pieces of cloth. The DNA reopened the conduit between witch and victim, forging a magical link that could be used to stop the witch's own urine. Added to the brew, according to an early recipe of 1671, were nails, pins or needles or tiny sharp bird bones, for a Molotov cocktail effect. The brew was stopped firm, wax-sealed and either concealed, often inverted, for as long as possible; like a lengthy imprisonment, this bottled up a witch's powers, rendering them useless. Alternatively, the bottles were heated to exploding point, to bring the witch a sudden, painful death.

The village crone

"In many of these cases, there had been antecedent personal quarrels, and so occasions of revenge; for some of those condemned, had been suspected by their neighbours several years, because after quarreling with their neighbours, evils had befallen those neighbours."

REV. JOHN HALE, CONTEMPORARY OF SALEM TRIALS

"Our cattle fall, our wives fall, our daughters fall, and maid-servants fall; and we ourselves shall not be able to stand if this beast be suffered to graze amongst us."

***THE WITCH OF EDMONTON*, WILLIAM ROWLEY, THOMAS DEKKER, JOHN FORD**

To some, the witch is not an outsider figure of supernatural power, but an embarrassing, powerless "doting old woman" (in the words of 16th-century unbeliever Reginald Scot), a scapegoat used to resolve the inevitable tensions that occur between neighbours. In close-knit communities, where we know each others' family histories, lives, loves and hates inside out, a demonized witch-figure may offer a legitimized way to resolve tension and prevent all-out conflict, and seems a particularly resonant option at times when communities begin to fracture. The historians Keith Thomas and Alan Macfarlane argue that this was true in the early modern era, when witchcraft accusations and trials peaked. This period saw the greatest social changes in millennia, as a close-knit, community-focused, agrarian way of life began to be replaced by a more individualistic, market-focused existence. The places where accusations of witchcraft were rife were successfully urbanizing civilizations, such as England, France and Germany.

Older women and those unable to work or without menfolk were particularly vulnerable as the old order crumbled—and there was a marked increased in widows and spinsters during this period. Previously, they had relied on the charity and goodwill of family or neighbours to get by, but as this informal social-support network broke down, and poverty became increasingly criminalized, they were regarded as a burden, even a threat to the new industrial order. Conflict was inevitable. If older women begged or harassed their neighbours for help and were rejected, tension and guilt grew on one side, envy and recrimination on the other, with angry words or muttered curses exchanged. If ill consequences followed—a child or animal fell ill, the butter failed to come—these were noted. There might be months, even years, of grumbling, hard feelings, bitching, gossip and harsh words behind hands and closed doors.

In his poem "The Three Graves" (*c.*1797), William Wordsworth makes his three thinly veiled witches stereotypical scapegoats: an aged mother, a barren wife and a forsaken maid. Abandoned by sons, husbands and suitors, all are easy subjects for malicious gossip. In Charles Dickens's *The Grey Woman* (1861), an abandoned young wife describes how the experience turns her into a witch-like supernatural creature:

> *There I lived in the same deep retirement, never seeing the light of day…my yellow hair was grey, my complexion was ashen-coloured, no creature could have recognized [me]…. They called me The Grey Woman.*

As the protagonist in the play *The Witch of Edmonton* states, she becomes:

> *a common sink*
> *For all the filth and rubbish of men's tongues*
> *To fall and run into.*

And then there was the matter of the land and property of these un-married old bags. In the early modern era, women accused of witchcraft who had no husbands, brothers or sons would forfeit their property, making them sitting targets for the unscrupulous.

In cases where there was much gossip and rumoured accusations of witchcraft, attempts were often made to smooth things over informally. Confrontations in public places were common; attempts to get an old lady to confess that she was a witch, make practical amends and undo a bewitching with the counter-magic of a muttered ritualized blessing. If an afflicted child or animal recovered, all might be well. But if this tactic failed—and once the whole community had come to a conclusion that this woman was indeed a witch—the matter might be taken further. Formal court sessions might be the last resort to rid a community of its social tensions. Those who turned on witches were, after all, sincere in their beliefs and perhaps only striving to make community life less stressful.

The Ducking of a Witch

They are fearful creatures, the witches! and yet I am sorry for the poor old women, whilst I dread them. We had one in Barford, when I was a little child. No one knew whence she came, but she settled herself down in a mud-hut by the common-side; and there she lived, she and her cat.... No one knew how she lived, if it were not on nettles and scraps of oatmeal and such-like food, given her more for fear than for pity. She went double, and always talking and muttering to herself. Folk said she snared birds and rabbits in the thicket that came down to her hovel. How it came to pass I cannot say, but many a one fell sick in the village, and much cattle died one spring, when I was near four years old. I never heard much about it, for my father said it was ill talking about such things; I only know I got a sick fright one afternoon, when the maid had gone out for milk and had taken me with her, and we were passing a meadow where the Avon, circling, makes a deep round pool, and there was a crowd of folk, all still—and a still, breathless crowd makes the heart beat worse than a shouting, noisy one. They were all gazing towards the water, and the maid held me up in her arms, to see the sight above the shoulders of the people; and I saw old Hannah in the water, her grey hair all streaming down her shoulders, and her face bloody and black with the stones and mud they had been throwing at her, and her cat tied round her neck. I hid my face, I know, as soon as I saw the fearsome sight, for her eyes met mine as they were glaring with fury—poor, helpless, baited creature!—and she caught the sight of me, and cried out, "Parson's wench, parson's wench, yonder, in thy nurse's arms, thy dad bath never tried for to save me; and none shall save thee, when thou art brought up for a witch." Oh! the words rang in my ears, when I was dropping asleep, for years after. I used to dream that I was in that pond; that all men hated me with their eyes because I was a witch: and, at times, her black cat used to seem living again, and say over those dreadful words.

***LOIS THE WITCH*, ELIZABETH GASKELL**

previous page: ***Woman Accused of Witchcraft*, Baldwin H. Ward and Kathryn C. Ward, 19th century, American**

A woman is accused of witchcraft. The female accuser more closely resembles the stereotype of a witch, with the half-moon profile and bony finger, suggesting that this is a community in crisis.

following page: ***The Ducking Stool*, Charles Stanley Reinhart, *c.*1870–1896, American**

An accused witch undergoing judgement. Water was considered a particularly accurate detector of witches, since they were held to have willfully rejected the sacred water of baptism.

Monstrous regiment

Fear of witches can be so great that after a purge of witches in two German villages in 1585, only one female in each was left alive. Cross-culturally and through time, witches have disproportionately been women. The estimated number of those executed as witches during "the burning times" (the witch hunts from the 15th to the early 18th centuries) varies wildly, from 40,000 to 9 million, the latter number popularized by the 19th-century suffragist Matilda Gage. But more than three-quarters were women, and a significant number of male witches were close relatives of accused females. What made witchcraft a female crime? Some commentators say a simple ratcheting up of society's all-pervasive misogyny, but a multitude of intertwining factors are at play. Witchcraft became thought of as a woman's crime—to men and women alike—because its misdemeanours took place on female turf (the home) and concerned female work: crimes were committed through foodstuffs (cooking) and potions (healing), by love and fertility magic (seduction and pregnancy), by harming children (childcare) and by cursing (story-telling). All who engaged in the ordinary daily tasks of the wife and mother were open to accusations of witchcraft.

The way in which witchcraft was prosecuted in the early modern era made it even more like women's business: many accusers were girls and women, and those who examined "witches" for evidence were licensed midwives. Women, were, of course, the root of evil for the Christian church. All daughters of Eve shared in her sin of collaborating with the devil. Trial evidence suggests that they were ready to confess it, too; woman seemed to believe that the voices in their heads telling them that they were bad mothers or nagging wives really were Satan. It's not so far-fetched. Most modern Western women half-believe the devil on the shoulder whispering that we're fat (or a bad mother).

Research suggests that age as well as gender marked out those accused of witchcraft. While women who spoke out against witches tended to come from one end of the fertility spectrum (aged between 11 and 20), those they pointed the finger at were from the other (elderly women, aged between 40 and 60). Women unable to support themselves in old age or whose family had left home were unsettling in an industrial society; if a woman's place is in the home, having no family to mother might be thought transgressive; and living to a great age might also suggest supernatural skill in times of poverty and disease.

Having a legitimate reason to abandon people who drain resources when society is under duress is important. Witchcraft provided it then and continues to do so even in the 21st century. Uncanny parallels can be seen in modern Africa, particularly in countries undergoing upheaval, such as South Africa, where villages have been established to provide sanctuary for people accused of witchcraft. If age is a burden in communities stricken by social and economic upheaval, so too is youth. In regions devastated by AIDS, it might be convenient to abandon orphans. Witchcraft is used to justify the act. In 2003, Save the Children claimed that of the 30,000 street children in Kinshasa, the capital of the Democratic Republic of Congo, virtually all had been accused of witchcraft. It noted that accusations rise dramatically when crops fail, the price of diamonds drops and jobs are lost. Blaming a witch can be the easiest option when a communal social support network breaks down.

The fascination of Salem

The execution of 14 women and five men for witchcraft (and the death of more, in jail or through torture), in Salem, Massachusetts in 1692–1693 has intrigued academics and theorists of popular culture perhaps more than any other period of witchcraft. The story started when the young daughter and the niece of the town's minister, Rev. Samuel Parris, began to exhibit strange symptoms: their bodies were contorted, they spoke in strange voices, objects flew around the room and they claimed to see demonic creatures and be stuck with pins. The doctor could find nothing physically wrong and diagnosed possession. Other girls began to experience similar symptoms, even during church meetings, and it was decided that there was a coven of witches at work in the town. Accused women were found to have dolls stuck with pins in their possession and, at first, fitted the description of the usual witch suspect: low born, slave, non-churchgoer. They were outsiders. But other suspects emerged who were pillars of the community and the church and were even male. It seemed that no one in the town was immune from the devil's influence. In just over a year, more than 150 had been arrested and jailed, often on "spectral evidence" obtained in dreams and visions. The court hearings were sensational, featuring the possessed girls centre-stage writhing on the floor and denouncing those brought before the court. The trials became so exhibitionist that they were halted in May 1693 and all the suspects still alive pardoned.

Since the 1970s, the amount of academic study and cultural exploration of this small community has been staggering. Explanations have been sought in the economic and social conditions of the village, the role of women and girls, and ways in which all three were changing;

in the contemporary court system, the organization of the church and factionalism in the town; crop failure, poverty and the changing nature of the post-agrarian world have been examined; internal causes have been sought, too, in hysteria, fear of Indian attacks and in the supernatural world the families inhabited; relations between the races have been found telling. But none can adequately explain why these events took place, nor why we find them so enthralling.

Perhaps the arts world can shed light where historical fact cannot penetrate. There have been numerous fictionalized accounts of the Salem witch phenomenon, from silent movies and graphic novels to episodes of *Sabrina the Teenage Witch*. The most notable remains Arthur Miller's play *The Crucible* (1953) because it helps to show why we are so intrigued by these events: they can help us to reflect on the anxieties of our own age. For Miller it was the scapegoating of the innocent by people in positions of power. The playwright's unstated focus was actually the 1950s activities of Senator Joseph McCarthy, who with his House Un-American Activities Committee persecuted, investigated and brought to trial many thousand Americans for supposed involvement in communist activities. Victims were imprisoned, blacklisted, lost their jobs and the respect of their communities. The most well-known of the harassment campaigns was conducted within the Holywood film community. The play helped to popularize the word "witch-hunt", which enabled us to think about and campaign against injustice. This may be the Salem witches' greatest legacy.

following page: *Edmund Cheeseman's Wife before Governor Berkeley*, Darley, *c.*1800, American

A 19th-century engraving shows a young suspect fainting before a judge during a witch trial as she points a finger at the accused, an elderly lady.

Exonerating the victims

Interview with Paula Gauthier Keene

In 1710, an amnesty was passed by the Massachusetts legislature that exonerated all those executed for witchcraft in Salem in 1692 whose families had petitioned to clear their names. But not all families were represented. Not until 2001 was a bill approved that cleared by name the remaining five victims: Susannah Martin, Bridget Bishop, Alice Parker, Margaret Scott and Wilmot Redd. The bill was passed thanks to the tireless campaigning of Salem teacher Paula Gauthier Keene. She is interviewed here by genealogist Sam Behling, descendant of two accused witches: Sarah Lord Wilson and her daughter, Sarah Wilson Jr.

Above: *View of Salem from Gallows Hill*, Alvan Fisher, 1818, British
The campaigner Paula Keene used to sit under this chestnut tree as a girl and imagine the lives of the 17th-century Salem witches.

Where does your passionate interest in the Salem witches come from?

"I was born in Salem and raised on Gallows Hills at the tippity top in a two family home at 10 Grafton Street. We had a panoramic sunrise view of downtown Salem and Salem Harbor from the Hill. My backyard was literally Gallows Hill Playground, a 22-acre parcel owned by the city of Salem.

Being an artist, I am introspective by nature. I have nourished a deep, mystical relationship with these victim souls ever since I can remember. My heart ached for them as a child and still aches for them as an adult. The fact that they died in my 'backyard' may have something to do with it? Their deaths seemed so unnecessary, I was always absorbed by the 'Whys?'.

Very early on in life, I could sense spirits and feel energies in and around Gallows Hill. I was never afraid of the Hill, I just always knew that my identity and destiny were somehow entwined with the Hill. It was like the Hill had a heartbeat of its own that I could feel pulsate in my blood. Wherever I went, the spirit of Gallows Hill came with me.

As a child, I would romp and run with the other children in the hills looking for the remains of shallow graves and dead men and women's bones. I would go over and over the pictures of my mother and her sisters in our family scrapbooks as they laid in the hills and posed by the "alleged" hanging tree when they were growing up. I built a replica of the Witch House for the sixth-grade history fair. I did book reports on Tituba. I read everything I could get my hands on at the local libraries about the Salem Witchcraft. Gallows Hill felt branded in my soul. Salem Witchcraft never left me alone.

The 20 deaths were always explained and best understood as the great enigmatic tragedy that they were. Growing up on Gallows Hill, I somehow carried an enigmatic stigma inside my own soul. I always knew that I was deeply connected to these people and nourished this fascination well into adulthood, trying to understand. Now, I understand that there's not a lot to understand about 'Hate Crimes' such as the mass execution of 20 in Salem. Hate is hate no matter what religious face it wears.

I even studied Witchcraft for a number of years myself and was taught by the Official Witch of Salem, Ms. Laurie Cabot in my spiritual quest. My knowledge of the Salem Witchcraft Hysteria was accompanied by my expanding knowledge of the Occult Arts and Sciences. When I took some graduate classes at Salem State College after the 1992 Salem Witchcraft Tercentenary Commemoration of 1692, I received the 'scholarly edge' that I needed to accompany my own life experiences with both contemporary and historical witchcraft. I never thought I would end up initiating legislation on Beacon Hill but mystery does love company and here we are at this point."

Do you feel a connection to any one of the five forgotten women?

"I always felt a deep soul-spirit, kindred sister-relationship with Bridget Bishop. In 1992 during the Tercentenary Commemoration, the mystical longing in my heart so grieved for her especially, that I had a Memorial Mass said for her at my church on the 300th anniversary of her June 10th death. We remembered her and the others in a kind of rest in peace prayer because she was the first to be executed on Gallows Hill. It wasn't until the graduate class research that I discovered that her 'attainder' [state of dishonour] was still on legal record. I was horrified by this discovery as my research led me into the Massachusetts Archives to validate my findings. Then after consulting a local attorney about my research, I knew the amendment legislation was in order and proceeded to set the exoneration wheels in motion."

Do you think such a memorial at Gallows Hill should be erected?

"I absolutely believe something needs to happen with Gallows Hill along the lines of a national monument. We, as a community continue to exploit the memory of the 20 people who were executed and the other 136 who were accused by portraying them to the world as something that they actually were not—real witches. Perpetuating this fictionalized account of witches and wizards over the centuries has overshadowed Salem's true identity and left this community with an inherited stigma. Must we continue to eclipse the truth into the new millennium? Or can we right some glaring historical wrongs? Those 20 victims who succumbed to execution upon Gallows Hill—20 who preferred death rather than admit to falsehood—were actually 20 of our nation's earliest martyrs. They died for the sake of the religious freedom that our latter-day American civil liberties were founded upon. The fact that they were Christians, not witches, shouldn't stand in the way of honouring them or memorializing the soil they died upon.

"The future heralds great hope for these victim souls. The dead, especially these five, should be honoured. Honour is one of the few things that is eternal. Let us finally give due honour to Bridget, Alice, Susannah, Wilmot and Margaret—five valiant martyrs who have waited over 300 years to be free. When I finally get to meet them in Heaven, I will be able to look them straight in the eyes and smile, knowing that I loved them in the best way I could on Earth."

Fear and loathing

The outsider may be cast in her role because her very appearance provokes feelings of disgust and revulsion. Witches are most often depicted as wrinkled, hook-nosed, wart-covered old crones with a harsh voice, stooped profile and withered, bony hands. Even those who pass as beautiful may be this way beneath the skin. Part of our awful reaction to her might derive from a seemingly innate human fear of ageing. Decay —whether in a lined face or senility—is something we seem hard-wired to find uncomfortable, and we learn to find it more unseemly in female than male form. The philosopher Mikhail Bakhtin regarded the epitome of the grotesque as a "senile, pregnant hag" (with a rich belly laugh). Maybe the discomfort we can feel around older women even stems from jealousy: clothed in grotesqueness, the witch can step outside the conventions that limit the way the rest of us look and behave. The women's health guru Dr. Christiane Northrup describes the rush of energy and outward-looking focus that many post-menopausal women experience when, for the first time since childhood, they are freed from the hormones that wire us for pregnancy and nurturing (the same freedom from hormones that contributes to the witch's appearance). They often use it, she says, to seize opportunities: changing career, launching a business, climbing mountains or runnning marathons. As rebel, outcast and malcontent, the witch can traverse the well-policed boundaries, leaving behind the kitchen and nursery to explore the great beyond.

"no one ever speaks of a 'beautiful old woman'"

***THE COMING OF AGE*, SIMONE DE BEAUVOIR**

The look of a witch

The typical witch of lore is defined by her messy, sluttish nature. She's not one for housework nor glossy personal grooming. She wears her long black locks tangled (or maybe entwined with snakes or other slithery familiars), her body parts are often deformed (perhaps a tail poking from beneath the hem of a skirt), her facial features distinctively worn or hooked. She oozes distortion and disruption of norms; a flip side to the sleekly groomed feminine norm. The sub-culture known as "Goth" (short for "gothic") adopts her style, and has cast a spell over teenagers since it first appeared in the late 1970s. Female icons from the punk movement warped a look and dress code from influences as diverse as *Frankenstein*'s monster bride, Morticia Addams, the floating gender of Weimar Germany's cabaret clubs, Victorian mourning dress and S&M corseting. Around the same time in the Netherlands and Italy, women protesting against sexual violence against women reclaimed the streets, marching under the slogan, "Fear and Tremble! Witches are back!" They drew on the protests of a decade earlier in New York, where radical feminists dressed as witches decided to reclaim the name witch, which they re-dubbed Women's International Terrorist Conspiracy From Hell.

The Goth look is a costume-department approach to dressing. It calls for a deathly pale complexion (the fake-tan celebrity look is strictly out), vampiresque blood-red nails and lips, blue-black hair and kohl-darkened eyes that command the authority of Cleopatra. This witch-inspired look is configured to empower its wearer—and scare off typical guys. By distortion, excess and historical references, the Goth frees herself from the male gaze to act in unexpected ways and move beyond boundaries. The look has drawn from high-fashion—the unstructured shapes, pleats and shades of black of Japanese designers—and influenced it. It can be seen in the unfinished, inside-out textures of Belgian 1990s deconstructivists and in Alexander McQueen's work: his spring/summer 2001 show featured models encased in straightjacket-tailoring with stuffed birds of prey and a swarm of giant moths.

Some Goths may embrace the witch's image because they identify with her outsider status; this is a subculture from insular suburbs and small towns, where those who choose a different path stand out. You might assume its fright value is negligible now the look is available off-the-peg in every US state (and Puerto Rico) from the chain store Hot Topic, but some garments are still controversial. In 1999, a school in New Mexico restricted the wearing of attire associated with "Gothic, satanic, or occult-type activities", including trench coats, knee-high boots, all-black clothing and spiked jewellery. And in 2007, a 20-year-old Goth, Sophie Lancaster, was attacked with her boyfriend while walking through a park in Bacup, Lancashire by a group of youths, who, the police later remarked, seemed motivated by the way in which the couple dressed. Both were left in a coma; Sophie died from her injuries.

previous page: **Detail from *Los Caprichos No 45: "There is plenty to suck"*, Francisco Goya, 1796–98, Spanish**

Because ugly old women are invisible in society, they are outlaws, free to do what they will. In Francisco de Goya's painting, this includes devouring infants. His is a satirical critique of superstition and prejudice during a time of political repression, economic crisis and clerical corruption.

The bad mother's club

The bad mother is the ultimate outsider, an icon of transgression subject to the scrutiny and judgment of friends and family, strangers in the supermarket and the apparatus of the state. When in 2006, American mom Brett Paesel wrote about how she got through numbingly dull days at home with pre-school children by using recreational drugs, afternoon cocktails and sex, she received the kind of opprobrium previously heaped on witches. The book was banned in Oregon and she was castigated by the press, psychologists and child-development specialists, but above all by outraged mothers. If we're looking for figures to mop up our anxieties about being a good-enough mother, the witch has been there since antiquity. Lamia, the Queen of Libya who became the child-murdering daimon, set the trend for monstrous mothers in Greek mythology—in Roman times and later, witches were known as *lamiae*—by roaming the globe every Full Moon sucking infants of their blood, then discarding them to their death. From then on, maternal cruelty was one of the defining features of women accused of witchcraft. In trials, witches were, over and again, accused of stealing infants (a crime that lingers from fairy changeling lore), harming children, and killing, dismembering or eating babies, like the legendary Baba Yaga. In the early modern era (some might say even today), if something happened to a child, it was assumed that the child's mother was a witch.

The witch is the flip side of the archetypal good mother. Hers is a dark, unnatural form of mothering. Her lullabies are curses and from her teat comes blood; she gives the fond nursery names of infants to her "imps", and instead of nursing to health, she can only support illness. Women accused of witchcraft in the early modern era seem, to us, only too willing to sign up to this notion. The devil or his spirits told them to do their dreadful deeds, they are quick to state. What else could explain such "unnatural" impulses? The daily conflicts of motherhood—the sleepless nights, the aching breasts, the poverty of time and money—bring with them tempting but terrible desires and impulses, and a good helping of self-disgust. The devil's gift to women in earlier eras was a language for expressing the anxieties of motherhood, and the unspeakable inner urges it can provoke, from suicide to infanticide—and a way of dealing with the guilt that followed. Embracing the devil brought a measure of absolution and a space in which to be heard and understood in their community. Some mothers accused of witchcraft would even be exonerated if they pledged to lead a more pious life. Today, similar anxieties and desires might be diagnosed and treated as symptoms of postnatal depression.

The devil also suggested some unpalatable but practical solutions in the days before social security or welfare payments. Studies of accused witches in 17th-century Essex show that most mothers charged with infanticide were unmarried girls, many servants with no way or place to look after a child. As we find in Lamia's story, infanticide is not the only sin, and it can be explained by circumstance, for Lamia's violent rage was provoked by Hera, the jealous wife of Lamia's lover Zeus. Hera killed Lamia's own children, and so traumatized is the witch that she can only rest in sleep by plucking out her own eyes.

previous page: **Modern Goths, Germany**

Fans of the New Wave and Gothic scene pictured at the M'era Luna Festival. German Goths at the alternative rock festival in Hildesheim are confident in the black corseting, lace and cat imagery associated with the witch.

Vor hexen nehmt
Seht! was sie mit

ch fein in acht,
n hänsel macht!

Hansel and Gretel's witches

In the Grimm Brothers' story of "Hansel and Gretel", the cruel mother figure is directly aligned with the witch in the forest. It is as if the first, the wicked stepmother, transforms into the second, for they are never in the same place at the same time, and when the children burn the witch, the mother exits the story too. The mother figure jumpstarts the story by insisting that the children are kicked out for eating the family out of house and home. It is her idea to take them deep into the forest and to abandon them. The father goes along with the plan.

Some readers see in the mother-witch combination a reflection of something all infants experience: the hateful, withholding mother. At the beginning of the 20th century, psychiatrist Sigmund Freud outlined how toddlers' perception of the mother shifts at around the age of two. They go from regarding her as the great, good provider—of food, comfort, warmth and locomotion—to the almighty withholder, who has the ability to bless them with these gifts, but chooses not to, forcing the child to walk, eat and sleep alone. Now he must begin to make his own way in the world and to see himself and his mother as separate beings. What a witch!

The child psychologist Bruno Bettleheim observed that Hansel and Gretel's witch performs this function for them, particularly for Gretel. She forces her to learn how to cook, clean and fetch water—the domestic duties that allow a girl to take her own place in the world. More than this, she teaches the children to use their ingenuity. When they first encounter the witch, they are innocent gluttons, falling on the edible house in the woods and eating it to destruction, as they have their parents' home. After Hansel is locked in the cage to be fattened up, they learn to bide their time, to fool the witch and after some weeks, have the wit not only to trick her into her own oven, but to uncover her hidden cache of jewels. But their true reward, forced on them unwillingly by two cruel mothers, is their own hidden treasure: their adult selves. Having located this gold, they can return home to their father and live happily ever after, especially now that Gretel's apprenticeship with the witch has equipped her to run the houschold.

We might remember that mothers usually read these tales to children. Might there not be some dark fantasies lurking within the images of the two witches? Such as the wish for small children to give us some space by learning to stand on their own two feet. When they can do this, both witch and mother are freed from the tale to pursue their own lives.

previous page: **Detail from *Hansel and Gretel*, Artist unknown, 19th century, German**

A detail from a mural found on the side of the "Hansel and Gretel House" in Oberammergau, Germany, a town famed for its houses painted with *Lüftlmalerei*, frescoes. The witch grasps Hansel in a bony grip while taunting poor Gretel. Scarily, this building is part of the town's orphanage.

following page: ***The Old Witch Combing Gerda's Hair*, Artist unknown, 19th century, British**

Gerda is lured into the old witch's home by a bowl of cherries. Although she is rather scared of the very old woman, Gerda allows herself to be lulled as the witch lovingly smoothes out her flaxen ringlets with a golden comb.

Good mother witch

In a number of fairy tales, the witch seems a kinder, more child-friendly figure than a child's true parents. In some, she becomes a surrogate mother, who has more concern for child protection. In the Brothers' Grimm story "Rapunzel", the parents are not only thieves, but willingly give away their baby girl at birth to a known witch. But the witch cares for Rapunzel so like a mother that she even nourishes the child in the womb, by assuaging the wife's pregnancy cravings. Later, around the time of puberty, she shuts the girl in an impregnable tower to keep her safe from the world, an impulse mothers of girls nearing puberty feel all too strongly. In Hans Christian Andersen's "Snow Queen", the strange old woman who "was not a wicked witch" but "conjured only a little for her own amusement," lures Gerda into her cottage with cherries, flowers and a bed with red silk pillows. The witch in the woods offers Hansel and Gretel similar treats: a sumptuous dinner of milk and sugared pancakes with apples and nuts, and two beautiful white beds. They feel "as if they have got into heaven". While Gerda eats, the woman combs her hair, a common form of conjuring used by fairy-tale witches to soothe their charges into an enchanted slumber, for all she wants—like the sorceress in Rapunzel—is for the "dear little maiden" to live with her forever.

following page: ***Rapunzel in her Tower*, Artist unknown, 19th century, British**
Rapunzel looks out of the tower in which she is imprisoned by the enchantress in this 19th-century illustration from *Grimms' Tales*. It lies in a forest and has neither stairs nor door; to ascend, the enchantress climbs the maid's magnificent long hair, fine as spun gold and just as strong.

An Enchanted Mother

Once upon a time there lived a man and his wife who were very unhappy because they had no children. These good people had a little window at the back of their house, which looked into the most lovely garden, full of all manner of beautiful flowers and vegetables; but the garden was surrounded by a high wall, and no one dared to enter it, for it belonged to a witch of great power, who was feared by the whole world.

One day the woman stood at the window overlooking the garden, and saw there a bed full of the finest rampion: the leaves looked so fresh and green that she longed to eat them. The desire grew day by day, and just because she knew she couldn't possibly get any, she pined away and became quite pale and wretched. Then her husband grew alarmed and said:

"What ails you, dear wife?"

"Oh," she answered, "if I don't get some rampion to eat out of the garden behind the house, I know I shall die."

The man, who loved her dearly, thought to himself, "Come! rather than let your wife die you shall fetch her some rampion, no matter the cost." So at dusk he climbed over the wall into the witch's garden, and, hastily gathering a handful of rampion leaves, he returned with them to his wife. She made them into a salad, which tasted so good that her longing for the forbidden food was greater than ever. If she were to know any peace of mind, there was nothing for it but that her husband should climb over the garden wall again, and fetch her some more. So at dusk over he got, but when he reached the other side he drew back in terror, for there, standing before him, was the old witch.

"How dare you," she said, with a wrathful glance, "climb into my garden and steal my rampion like a common thief? You shall suffer for your foolhardiness."

"Oh!" he implored, "pardon my presumption; necessity alone drove me to the deed. My wife saw your rampion from her window, and conceived such a desire for it that she would certainly have died if her wish had not been gratified." Then the Witch's anger was a little appeased, and she said:

"If it's as you say, you may take as much rampion away with you as you like, but on one condition only—that you give me the child your wife will shortly bring into the world. All shall go well with it, and I will look after it like a mother."

The man in his terror agreed to everything she asked, and as soon as the child was born the witch appeared, and having given it the name of Rapunzel, which is the same as rampion, she carried it off with her.

Rapunzel was the most beautiful child under the sun. When she was 12 years old the witch shut her up in a tower, in the middle of a great wood, and the tower had neither stairs nor doors, only high up at the very top a small window. When the old witch wanted to get in she stood underneath and called out:

"Rapunzel, Rapunzel,
Let down your golden hair."

For Rapunzel had wonderful long hair, and it was as fine as spun gold. Whenever she heard the Witch's voice she unloosed her plaits, and let her hair fall down out of the window about twenty yards below, and the old Witch climbed up by it.

"RAPUNZEL", THE BROTHERS GRIMM, *THE RED FAIRY BOOK,* (ED.) ANDREW LANG

Grandmother witch

In Hans Christian Anderson's tale "The Snow Queen", Gerda reminds us that grannies have extraordinary and ancient powers that the young in the world often neglect to cultivate. Hers, says Gerda wistfully, is an animal whisperer: "my grandmother understands it [the language of the animals], and used to speak it to me. I wish I had learned it." By cultivating our grandmothers, we safeguard a repository of knowledge that can help us to understand and negotiate the world. If we choose not to, they are there for us in the end anyway; in the underworld lives the Germanic witch Hulda, also known as the Dark Grandmother, who looks after babies and children who have died.

We all have two grandmothers; this note of duality hints at the ambiguities ripe for exploration in the figure of the grandmother. Lurking beneath the surface of the good granny may be a more ambiguous outsider; maybe, like Red Riding Hood's grandmother, a wolf under the mob cap and spectacles, ready to upset your DNA load—or eat you up. After all, the witch and the werewolf do share the woods at night.

"The Snow Queen" offers us another image of the child-eating outsider granny: the bearded, drink-sodden old robber woman, who licks her lips and draws a shining blade when she imagines how sweet little Gerda will taste.

But equally, witch grannies who seems superficially terrifying might not be so evil. The Russian witch Baba Yaga—*baba* means "peasant woman" or "granny" and *yaga* "witch"—is a child-eating old hag with a fearsome temper and countenance. But if treated with respect and served well she may reward. Vasilisa the Beautiful, despite being filled with horror, displays bravery, politeness and resourcefulness, and does

all required of her by the old witch: cleaning, sweeping, cooking, sorting, and not complaining. Baba Yaga fits her for a good marriage.

Resourcefulness is the key to making the best of a grandmother witch. In a tale from Kolyma in Siberia, told in 1895, when the she-monster Yaghishna stalks into a home, the mother and father run off, leaving their small girl in swaddling clothes in the bed. Yaghishna eventually finds the infant and bursts her bonds. Following a few slaps from the witch, the infant gains the strength to carry water, chop wood and make a fire. So empowered is the tiny girl that she liberates the witch's reindeer and escapes her, causing the old hag to drink herself to death at a river in an attempt to reach the girl on the opposite bank. After her belly bursts, the child takes the witch's body and forms from it everything she needs to live an independent life: the witch's head becomes her cup, her fingers forks, her joints and buttocks supports for her home and mortar, and her legs and backbone a scraper and scraping board. If we are brave enough, we can take on the witch's outsider powers and use them to fuel our future.

left: *Baba Yaga*, D. Mitrokhin, 1915, British

Baba Yaga beats with her pestle and sweeps with her besom to propel herself across the sky. Her arms are powerfully sinewy yet she has no flesh on her legs in Dimitry Mitrokhin's illustration.

Good Granny, Bad Granny

"Dear children," she said to the orphans, "go to my grandmother who lives in the forest in a hut on hen's feet. You will do everything she wants you to, and she will give you sweet things to eat and you will be happy."

The orphans started out. But instead of going to the witch, the sister, a bright little girl, took her brother by the hand and ran to their own old, old grandmother and told her all about their going to the forest.

"Oh, my poor darlings!" said the good old grandmother, pitying the children, "my heart aches for you, but it is not in my power to help you. You have to go not to a loving grandmother, but to a wicked witch. Now listen to me, my darlings," she continued; "I will give you a hint: Be kind and good to everyone; do not speak ill words to any one; do not despise helping the weakest, and always hope that for you, too, there will be the needed help."

The good old grandmother gave the children some delicious fresh milk to drink and to each a big slice of ham. She also gave them some cookies—there are cookies everywhere—and when the children departed she stood looking after them a long, long time.

The obedient children arrived at the forest and, oh, wonder! there stood a hut, and what a curious one! It stood on tiny hen's feet, and at the top was a rooster's head. With their shrill, childish voices they called out loud:

"Izboushka, Izboushka! turn thy back to the forest and thy front to us!"

The hut did as they commanded. The two orphans looked inside and saw the witch resting there, her head near the threshold, one foot in one corner, the other foot in another corner, and her knees quite close to the ridge pole.

"Fou, Fou, Fou!" exclaimed the witch; "I feel the Russian spirit."

The children were afraid, and stood close, very close together, but in spite of their fear they said very politely:

"Ho, grandmother, our stepmother sent us to thee to serve thee."

"All right; I am not opposed to keeping you, children. If you satisfy all my wishes I shall reward you; if not, I shall eat you up."

Without any delay the witch ordered the girl to spin the thread, and the boy, her brother, to carry water in a sieve to fill a big tub. The poor orphan girl wept at her spinning-wheel and wiped away her bitter tears.

"BABA YAGA", *FOLK TALES FROM THE RUSSIAN*,
VERRA XENOPHONTOVNA KALAMATIANO DE BLUMENTHAL

following page: ***The Girl and Baba Yaga*, Edouard Zier, 1904, French**
Inside the hut of Baba Yaga the girl serves the grandmother well; she will thrive in her company. Note the super-sized pestle and mortar in the hearth ready to carry Baba Yaga on her nocturnal expeditions.

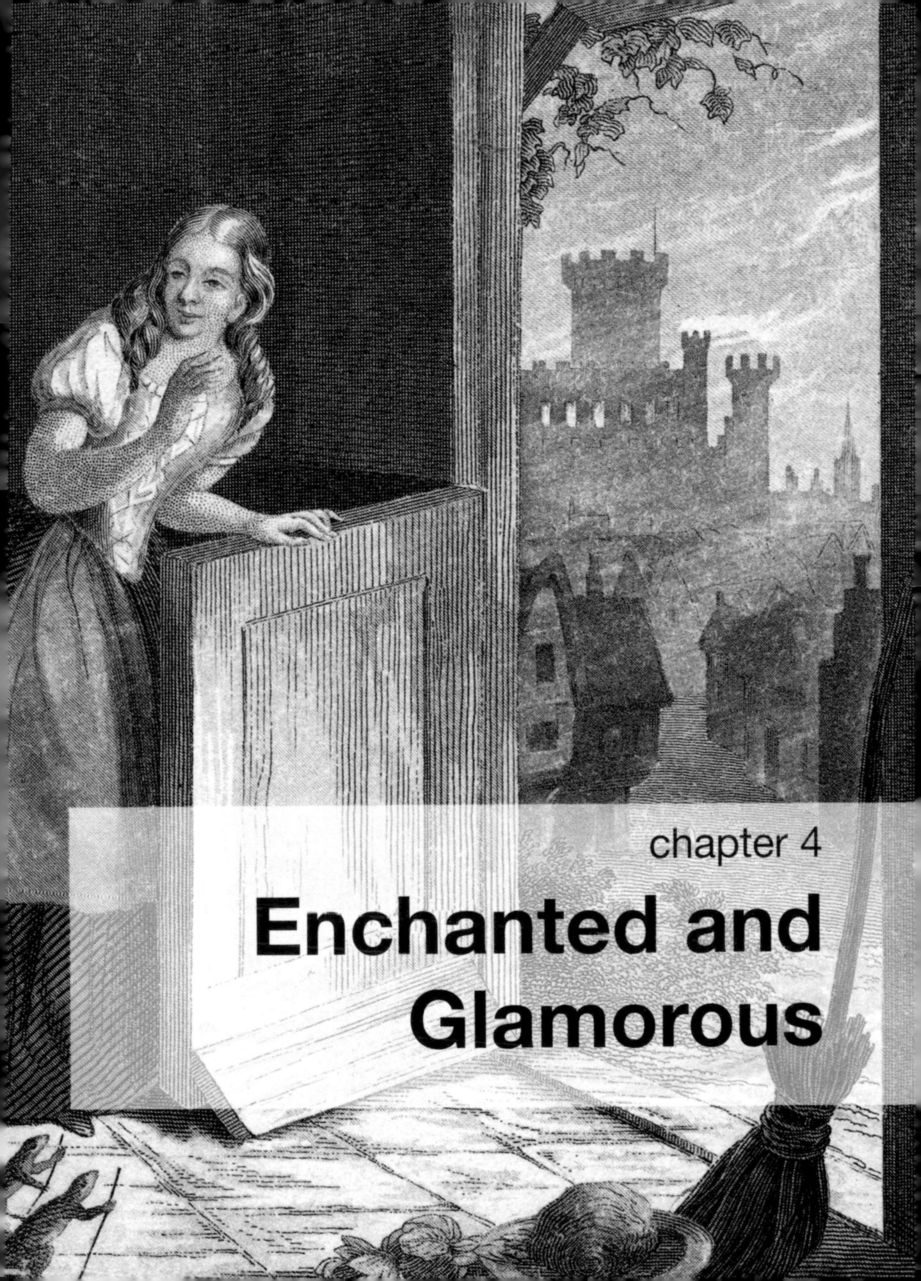

chapter 4

Enchanted and Glamorous

The glamorous witch

With her supernatural powers the witch can choose to enthral people and possessions and direct the forces of nature to do her will. Her power extends equally over the mighty and the low-born: kings and queens have believed themselves bewitched, mortals in the robust health, and those so young they are still in the womb. For people on the margins, this might be a very desirable fantasy—one perhaps worth cultivating—for even to be thought of as a witch is to claim some of her extraordinary powers.

The witch has command over healing—she can bring on or ease minor ailments, from sprains to burns and toothache, and major illness—and may assist or hinder fertility, pregnancy and childbirth. She can cast a circle of protection around those in peril on the sea, out hunting or at court, and guard precious farm animals against misfortune—or entwine them in storm and discord. She can look into the future or the past, find lost fortunes and determine the course of love. To achieve these ends, witches call on many forms of magic: words of enchantment and magic numbers; the forces of the planets, directions and elements; scrying techniques and spell-lore. In the English ballad "Alison Gross", the narrator who resists a witch's advances—she is, after all, "The ugliest witch in the north country"—is punished by an battery of weapons. Turning spells, the number three, the Moon and stars, curses and word spells; all are directed at him from a silver wand. No surprise, then, that the poor man falls paralyzed to the ground and can only be revived by the fairy queen herself.

But the greatest of the witch's powers is not hers to wield. It is in the heads of others. It's not what these women do, necessarily, that gives them magic potential, but what others believe they do, a belief that must be solid in a community from top to bottom for an accusation of witchcraft to hold. So ingrained is the supernatural still in our way of thinking about the world that it shows through in the words we use to describe the unexplainable (including our inner state and raw emotions). We might refer to our guardian angel or inner demons, speak of being possessed, of monstrous urges and fiendish desires, of feeling haggard.

William Wordsworth puts it deftly in his poem "Goody Blake and Harry Gill". No one in the piece accuses the eponymous Goody—an impoverished old lady who lives on a hill—of being a witch, but when Harry, the "lusty drove", finds her out on a bone-crushing frosty night pulling sticks from his hedge to fuel her fire, that is his unstated conclusion. So sure is he of her status and therefore her powers, that when he attacks her, he interprets her mumbled prayer as a curse. Sure enough, on the morrow, his flesh starts to "fall away" and he takes to his bed forever. The imagination can make fears flesh; a most witchlike process. As another of Wordsworth's hags, the aged widow in "The Three Graves", taunts: "I am a woman weak and old, Why turn a thought on me?"

previous page: ***Cinderella with Fairy Godmother in the Kitchen*, Artist unknown, Date unknown**

In an illustration to Perrault's tales, Cinderella looks on as her diminutive fairy godmother works her magic. The kitchen cauldron bubbles away merrily, as if to emphasize the witch-like powers of transformation.

SIR. LAVNCELOT.
AND. THE. WITCH.
HELLAWES.

"Away, away you ugly witch
Hold far away and let me be
For I wouldna aince kiss your ugly mouth
For all the gifts that you could gi'.

She's turned her right and round about,
And thrice she blew on a grass-green horn;
And she swore by the moon and the stars aboon,
That she'd gar me rue the day I was born.

Then out she's taken a silver wand,
And she's turned her three times round and round;
She's mutter'd such words, that my strength it fail'd,
And I fell down senseless on the ground."

"ALISON GROSS", ENGLISH BALLAD

left: ***Sir Launcelot and the Witch Hellawes*, Aubrey Beardsley, 19th century, British**

Aubrey Beardsley's woodcut from an 1893 edition of Sir Thomas Malory's *Le Morte d'Arthur* shows that a knight must be on his guard. It is not only the ingredients of a potion that might leave a hero spellbound, the very presence of a sorceress can be enough to overcome the mighty.

A family profession?

From Greek mythology to the TV series *Charmed*, witchcraft is thought to be a skill one is born with. It may have passed through generations down the female line or materialize as a consequence of an unusual birth: being the seventh child of a seventh child, emerging foot-first or with unusual birthmarks, red hair or webbed fingers. Those with a mother or sister known to be a witch during the "burning times" were more likely to be accused themselves. Inference of this type was heady: accusations that King Henry VIII's wife Anne Boleyn was a witch were used to indirectly slander her daughter, Queen Elizabeth I. This is still the way in cultures around the globe that believe in maleficium. In 2006, a tea plantation worker from the Adivasi community in Assam state, north-east India, who had a reputation as a traditional healer, was beheaded for allegedly causing an epidemic of illness and death. To rid the community of his influence, four of the family's children were killed, too.

Because it is inherited from a mother or grandmother, the craft might be compared to a domestic skill essential for sustaining life. Charms and spells borrow from recipe templates and cross over with sewing, cooking, cleaning and nursing techniques. But like these skills, too, the craft can be acquired. Characters in the TV series *Buffy the Vampire Slayer* make their way by following formulae in spell-books. Some of the stories that emerge from the witchcraft trials suggest that "ordinary" women took the first steps along the path by "borrowing" a simple charm to ward off a physical affliction, such as aching joints. If the spell worked and was seen to work by others she might pass on the words or instructions, which helped to build her

reputation for spell-craft. It's a slippery slope; often these stories are presented like tabloid morality tales warning that the odd joint leads to an addiction to crack cocaine.

Charmers set themselves apart from witches, considering their gifts to be God-given and something they should pass on without payment to aid those who suffer. Their charms were often communicated down the family line by a whisper on the death bed, and largely concerned cures for injury and ailments, such as burns, warts and ringworm. Some might only be effectual on someone of the opposite sex, but many worked for humans and animals alike. Charmers might choose to work with their hands rather than words, a gift so highly prized that it was considered the provenance of monarchs, conferred by God on legitimate rulers only.

A CHARM TO GAIN ADVANTAGE OF A MAN OF SUPERIOR STRENGTH

"I [name] breathe upon thee. Three drops of blood I take from thee: the first out of thy heart, the other out of thy liver, and the third out of thy vital powers; and in this I deprive thee of thy strength and manliness."

previous page: ***Los Caprichos No 6: Pretty Teacher*, Francisco Goya, 1786–1798, Spanish**

In Goya's *Los Caprichos No 6* an older witch teaches a younger how to fly. The piece was regarded as a thinly veiled comment on prostitution in 18th-century Spanish society.

A power struggle

The witch emerged as a figure of populist concern at a time when the church in Europe was undergoing considerable change. In late medieval Europe, religious wars were raging and dissent rising as disasters and disease shook people's faith; hierarchies in the church as well as in society and families were being renegotiated in urbanizing countries such as France, Germany and England; and new forms of worship offered direct access to God rather than through church elders. It must have felt like a dangerous world to church leaders. They were also losing their control of the supernatural domain, as philosophers, doctors, scientists and mathematicians offered new ways of understanding the unseen. In the past, the priest's supernatural rites had defended life from birth to death, and his blessings shielded the day and the week.

But now spiritual crises could be read as medical symptoms or settled in a secular court; and ill fortune that came out of nowhere explained by physics or inventions such as the telescope. This spread anxiety about the role of God, and doubt in the authority vested in His church.

The church embraced the witch because in an age of increasing uncertainty she proved one thing for sure—that God existed. If a witch confessed to consorting with demons (especially in an intensely physical way, such as in sex), then there must be angels and there must be a God. Having demons abroad brought people back to their faith and the strong arms of the church.

The use of spells is so widespread among the people here that not a man or woman begins, undertakes, does or refrains from doing anything…without employing some particular blessing, incantation, spell, or other such heathenish means… Whenever an article of clothing has been mislaid and cannot be found, when someone feels sickly or a cow acts queer, they run at once to the soothsayer to ask who has stolen it or put a bad spell on it, and to fetch some charm to use against the enchanter…”

LUTHERIAN INSPECTORS OF WEISBADEN, GERMANY, 1594

Magic makes the world go round

With a belief in witchcraft come a neat explanation for disorder and disaster: bad fortune is the work of evil-doers with access to the way the Universe works. If this is true, you can do something about it; perhaps exclude them from community life, propitiate them for good fortune, or adopt and adapt some of their measures. Before the Reformation, all manner of lore abounded to ward off misfortune, from thieves to disease, and to bring about a change in circumstance. Though it involved folk practices, this form of magic was largely sanctioned by the church and relied on church paraphernalia for its psychic potency: candles, rosaries and the crucifix, icons and statues of saints, holy water and wafers, and prayers in the sacred language, Latin.

After the Reformation, openly Catholic "superstition" was discouraged by the new Protestant churches. But it was still used illicitly. Gone underground and self-administered, over generations the half-remembered Latin masses and paternosters were recast and blended with astrological language; storytelling narrative devices were added; alliteration, repetition and rhyme riffed on, and acts of sympathetic magic woven in. Out of place and out of time, these quasi-religious charms were regarded as evidence of witchcraft, but were widely used. In 1594, the Lutherian inspectors in Weisbaden, Germany, reported how everyone they encountered used word charms and rhymes, whether they understood them or not. They remarked that holy names were especially popular: the names of God,

the Holy Trinity, archangels and saints, the holy virgin, twelve apostles and three kings. Saints have long associations with curative powers. Being protectors or patrons of specific spheres of life or professions and associated with Bible stories, each one could be invoked for help in curing a particular illness: Peter for fishing and toothache, Paul for snakebite, George for cattle, John the Baptist for headaches (he was beheaded!), Martha for fevers. Using a name is, of course, a sure way to call up a spirit and in some cultures still, it is thought best not to use the name of the deceased for this reason.

CHARM FOR THE TOOTHACHE

"Christ passed by his brother's door,
Saw Peter his brother lying on the floor;
What aileth thee, brother?
Pain in thy teeth?
Thy teeth shall pain thee no more:
In the name of the Father, Son, and Holy Ghost.
Amen."

ENGLISH HEALING CHARM

left: ***An Incantation Scene*, Frans Francken the Younger, 17th century, Flemish**

All manner of manifestations are drawn down by the witches and the artist: the inexplicable, the mysterious, the Gothic and the deviant. No doubt the witches employed quasi-religious charms in their spell books.

Superstition in Salem

There was much to tell upon the imagination in those days, in that place and time. It was prevalently believed that there were manifestations of spiritual influence—of the direct influence both of good and bad spirits—constantly to be perceived in the course of men's lives. Lots were drawn, as guidance from the Lord; the Bible was opened and the leaves allowed to fall apart; and the first text the eye fell upon was supposed to be appointed from above as a direction. Sounds were heard that could not be accounted for; they were made by the evil spirits not yet banished from the desert-places of which they had so long held possession. Sights, inexplicable and mysterious, were dimly seen—Satan, in some shape, seeking whom he might devour. And, at the beginning of the long winter season, such whispered tales, such old temptations and hauntings and devilish terrors, were supposed to be peculiarly rife. Salem was, as it were, snowed up, and left to prey upon itself. The long, dark evenings; the dimly lighted rooms; the creaking passages, where heterogeneous articles were piled away, out of the reach of the keen-piercing frost, and where occasionally, in the dead of night, a sound was heard, as of some heavy falling body, when, next morning, everything appeared to be in its right place (so accustomed are we to measure noises by comparison with themselves, and not with the absolute stillness of the night-season); the white mist, coming nearer and nearer to the windows every evening in strange shapes, like phantoms—all these, and many other circumstances: such as the distant fall of mighty trees in the mysterious forests girdling them round; the faint whoop and cry of some Indian seeking his camp, and unwittingly nearer to the white man's settlement than either he or they would have liked, could they have chosen; the hungry yells of the wild beasts approaching the cattle-pens—these were the things which made that winter life in Salem, in the memorable time of 1691–1692, seem strange, and haunted, and terrific to many; peculiarly weird and awful to the English girl, in her first year's sojourn in America.

***LOIS THE WITCH*, ELIZABETH GASKELL**

An Irish-American Witch, 1668

Four children of John Goodwin in Boston which had enjoyed a Religious Education, and answer'd it with a towardly Ingenuity; Children indeed of an exemplary Temper and Carriage, and an Example to all about them for Piety, Honesty, and Industry. These were in the year 1688 arrested by a stupendous Witchcraft. The Eldest of the children, a Daughter of about Thirteen years old, saw fit to examine their Laundress, the Daughter of a Scandalous Irish Woman in the Neighbourhood, whose name was Glover…about Some Linnen that was missing, and the Woman bestowing very bad language on the Child, in the Daughter's Defence, the Child was immediately taken with odd Fits, that carried in them something Diabolical. It was not long before one of her Sisters, with two of her Brothers, were horribly taken with the like Fits, which the most Experienc'd Physicians…pronounced Extraordinary and preternatural; and one thing the more confirmed them in this Opinion was, that all the Children were tormented still just the

same part of their Bodies, at the same time, though their Pains flew like swift lightning from one part to another, and they were kept so far asunder that they neither saw nor heard each other's Complaints. At nine or ten a-clock at Night they still had a Release from their miseries, and slept all Night pretty comfortably. But when the Day came they were most miserably handled. Sometimes they were Deaf, sometimes Dumb, and sometimes Blind, and often all this at once. Their tongues would be drawn down their throats, and then pull'd out upon their Chins, to a prodigious Length. Their Mouths were forc'd open to such a Wideness, that their jaws were out of joint; and anon clap together again, with a Force like a Springlock: and the like would happen to their Shoulder-blades, their Elbows and Handwrists, and several of their joints.... Their Necks would be broken, so that their Neck-bone would seem dissolv'd unto them that felt after it, and yet on the sudden it would become again so stiff, that there was no stirring of their Heads; yea, their Heads would be twisted almost round. And if the main Force of their Friends at any time obstructed a dangerous Motion which they seemed upon, they would roar exceedingly.

***IRISH WITCHCRAFT AND DEMONOLOGY*, ST. JOHN D. SEYMOUR, B.D.**

previous page: ***Hanging of Bridget Bishop*, Artist unknown, 18th century, American**

Bridget Bishop was the first woman to be executed as a witch in the Salem outbreak of 1692. Her lifestyle helped to seal her reputation to church and community: she was known to live extravagantly, dress in a showy manner and disregard the moral standards of the day.

The devil's language

Speaking "other" languages was a sign of the witch. It's notable that the supposed last fluent speaker of Cornish in Cornwall was accused of being a witch not just for her knowledge of other worlds, but for her preferred tongue. Dolly Pentreath, a fishwife from Mousehole who died in 1777 aged 102, held a reputation as a wise woman with "weird" powers. Her colourful use of language and feisty temper, her independence and eccentric demeanour only enhanced her status, bringing villagers to her door. Stories describe Dolly single-handedly chasing a navy press gang out of her village with a hatchet and a mouthful of ripe curses. A favourite was to call people *kronnekyn hager du*, "ugly black toad". She would often be seen cursing passing fishermen from her seat in the Keigwin Arms nursing a pipe and a pint of ale. According to legend, her last words were, *Me ne vidn cewsel Sawznek!* ("I don't want to speak English!") All over Europe after the Reformation, Basques, Corsicans, Bretons, Alsatians, Provençaux and Catalans among others lost their languages of ancient power to those of a unified nation state. Outlawed through centralized institutions and the education system, national tongues were abandoned by the young and became associated with barbarism, outmoded values and vulgar old ladies. Theirs were shameful words, only spoken in private. But this difference gave women such as Dolly Pentreath considerable influence and the force to disturb and disrupt the regular world.

following page: ***The Witch Number 3*, George H. Walker, 1892, American**

This lithograph by George H. Walker & Co. after Joseph E. Baker depicting the Salem trials, the accused witch's literal power over words is apparent.

Word magic

Through word spells, a witch bring things to pass. She turns words—marks made on paper or in the air, on water or holy bread, or by a movement of the mouth, tongue and respiratory system—into realities, using them to manifest objects or physical states, make people behave in a particular way or to travel through space and time. A Russian witch might intone them like a priest, murmur them, breathe her powerful words over the recipient or speak them for the wind to carry, in a manner similar to the prayer flags of Tibet. This act of creation replicates the work of a creator god who brings the world into being through words. Hindus believe that the sacred syllable OM is the source of everything that is; Muslims that the name Allah contains all the qualities that give rise to the Universe; Christians that "In the beginning was the Word and the Word was with God, and the Word was God" (John 1:1). Some derivations of names for witches hint at this divine power—in the Basque country, a witch might be known as *sorginak*, perhaps from the root of the verb "to create".

The great religions teach that mankind is innately divine—we are made in the form of God—and that by uttering holy words we reanimate this holy spirit within. The mouth and tongue are regarded as the temple

right: *Wicked Fairy Casting a Spell on Sleeping Beauty*, Artist unknown, early 20th century, British

The power of a curse and a pointing finger expressed in an illustration of the Sleeping Beauty's christening celebration from the 1890s. Most of the fairies come dressed as bright young ladies of the court. Only their sister, the wicked fairy, appears in the guise of an elderly witch.

gate, the place where we begin to express our divinity, especially if we choose to utter words from languages thought to have been divinely revealed, such as Latin and Arabic. Such holy words—divinity encased in a sound structure—offer a path to self-realization, absorption in God and the kingdom of Heaven. By knowingly garbling those words or directing their innate power for ill means—by uttering anti-prayers—as the witch in history is reputed to have done, she proclaims her status as a heretic.

Word charms and rhymes have particular charge in an oral culture, and the written word was a thing of awe in the days when most people couldn't write, especially if it included holy words. Spells would be written on scraps of paper or, more auspiciously, inscribed into "virgin" parchment cured from the hide of unborn animals. These could be rolled up and slotted into amulets, placed over parts of the body that required healing or even eaten. For those who believe enough, ingesting words of power can be a mighty placebo.

"Her lippes ever chattering and walking: but no man knew what."

DESCRIPTION OF ANNE WHITTLE, PENDLE WITCH, GERMANY, 1612

Thrice round the Moon

Magical numbers are often repeated in bewitching charms as a means of tapping into concealed wisdom. Three is the number most commonly used in spells, as a triple repetition of rhymes and names. Three is charged by a number of powerful trinities: it is birth, death and rebirth; maiden, mother, crone; mind, body and spirit; father, mother, child—and much more. Many religions have sacred trinities, the ancient Greek, Hindu, Inca and Chinese deities among them. Three is considered the most complete or harmonious number for having a beginning, middle and end, and in physical form it is represented by the shamrock, *triskel*, the triangular formation within crosses and the Chinese trigram. Nine is all the more powerful for being three times three—a Wiccan circle is often nine feet in diameter—and three nines, too, hold great potency.

Having knowledge of magic numbers confers authority over space, given the relationship between numbers and geometry. Shapes with a magical charge include the triangle, a protective shape often used in weavings and embroidery to deflect evil intent with its three sharpened points. But more often associated with witches is the five-pointed shape that contains triangle magic within its form: the star or pentagram. Five has been called the figure of life, or soul, because it lies at the heart of the number system, and so holds the energetic charge of the Universe and its power-source, the Sun. It weds the number two (the masculine and worldly) with three (the feminine and spiritual). A pentagram can be drawn with one unbroken line (as in knot magic) with the uppermost point heading skyward—if you then go on to describe a circle around it, you draw a pentacle. In this form, the star resembles a human body with four limbs and a head, or it might be thought to stand for the five senses. It also suggests equilibrium between the elements earth, water, fire, air and ether, or spirit. A five-pointed star has been used as a symbol for worship since ancient times and by different faiths. The earliest suggested use is as a symbol of the goddess Kore, also worshipped as the Roman goddess Ceres, who presides over nature, and it can be seen if you cut through the equator of an apple, at the "core". Some suggest that the shape traces the movements of the planet associated with another goddess, Venus. When inverted, the pentagram, the most holy and benign of symbols, representing mankind's access to mystical powers, has two points, or horns, ascendant and is associated with Satan.

TUSCAN WITCH'S INCANTATION, TO BE SPOKEN INTO A SHELL

"There are three sounds, and one
Of them I fain would hear:
The crow of a cock,
A dog barking for me,
The mew of a cat
If one of the three
I shall clearly hear, "twill be a sign
That what I seek shall ere long be mine!""

***ETRUSCAN ROMAN REMAINS IN POPULAR TRADITION*, CHARLES GODFREY LELAND**

Enchanted circle

As part of their rites, most modern practitioners of the craft consecrate a circle, or its three-dimensional form, a sphere, by describing its shape in the air or on the earth using a ritual sword or knife, the *athame*. The circle will be purified by calling on the elements and by lighting candles to honour the four cardinal directions. The space within a cast circle is a sacred place of protection: a circle has no beginning and no end; there is no way out and no way in. Since from its sacred central point every other part of the circle is equidistant, the shape represents unity and perfection. It also recalls the womb where life grows, the power of the Full Moon and the Sun, the dome of the sky seen from the Earth, the globe and the wheel of the seasons and so time everlasting. A cast and purified circle is a place of confined sacred energy that stands outside time and space; indeed it is sometimes pictured as a cylinder or cone that extends heavenward, connecting our realm with others. There can be no more powerful place to cast spells.

following page: **Greenham Common, Main Gate, Edward Barber, October 1982, British**

Rebecca Johnson, on the left, obstructing building work at the main gate.

Peace Magic

Interview with Dr. Rebecca Johnson

Dr. Rebecca Johnson is a peace activist; she spent five years at the peace camp at the Greenham Common nuclear base in the 1980s—and is a member of the International Institute for Strategic Studies (IISS) and Women in Black, a world-wide network of women committed to peace and justice. She is a former Vice Chair of the Board of the *Bulletin of the Atomic Scientists* and from 2004 to 2006 was senior advisor to the Weapons of Mass Destruction Commission chaired by Dr. Hans Blix. She also serves on the advisory councils of the Centre for Policy Studies (Moscow), the Peace Depot (Japan), the UK All-Party Parliamentary Group on Global Security and Non-Proliferation, and the Oxford Research Group (UK). She co-founded the Acronym Institute for Disarmament Diplomacy in 1995 and lectures to a wide range of UN and other international conferences.

How did the women's peace movement come to be associated with witches?

I was a political animal when I went to Greenham Common; I saw it as a way to bring large numbers of women together to take action for peace. But a number of women there had a spiritual angle on protest. They had read the feminist theologian Mary Daly and looked at Goddess religions. We found out that one of the last witches to be condemned to death, the Newbury Witch, had been based on Greenham Common. There was a sense that the pogroms against witches targeted women who didn't conform to being subservient to men. These were women who lived on their own and had knowledge of plants that cure and the way the female body works; it's no accident that attacks against witches took place at a time when men were subjecting all knowledge to the prism of male ways of thinking. These women knew how plants had effect through observation and passed-on knowledge, but lacked the ability to explain how healing worked; they couldn't put it into a language that made sense to men because they didn't have the tools of reading or Latin. Theirs was a different kind of intelligence. For us, there was a parallel at Greenham. We knew that the arguments for nuclear weapons were purile. We knew in our sinews and with every sense that nuclear weapons would not make the world more secure, but were constantly pilloried as well-meaning but stupid by supercilious men; "If you knew what we knew" was the inference, "you'd stop your protest". Even the men in the early

80s peace movement—the academics and priests—assumed they had all the answers. Having worked as an adviser to Hans Blix, I now have that privileged knowledge. I know what was going on in the 80s, and we were right.

What particularly "female" methods did you use in your protests?

In witches you see women who have an independent power; a different kind of knowledge. Our way of exerting this power was to actively ridicule the military. For example, we would dress up as giant pink teddy bears to enter the nuclear base. And when they took out weapons on huge dark green conveys that were supposed to "melt into the countryside", we would throw what we called "gloop" over them—a mixture of porridge and pink paint. The colour pink was key; we were using its associations with femininity and queerness to ridicule the deep, dark masculinity of the convoys. Then there was the act of stirring it in a cauldron! Gloop was rather effective; it stopped the trucks and drove the military round the bend. Most women know what a nightmare it is to scrape stuck-on porridge off pans, so imagine how much more difficult it is if mixed up with pink paint. We'd gloop them just outside the base. They couldn't stop immediately; that would be too humiliating, so they'd carry on, with men detailed to spend time cleaning off the set-on gloop on arrival. Then we'd gloop them on the way back in. Consciously ridiculing was a transgressive power that made the establishment fear us.

Tell me about the encircling of the camp in 1982, when tens of thousands of women came together to Embrace the Base—to clasp hands around the perimeter fence. Casting a circle is one of the most potent images associated with the power of a witch.

I was at the meeting when we first decided to embrace the base: to encircle the site with women. Part of the idea was to get lots of women to turn up, but we also saw the encircling as a form of power—an act of love that could contain and diffuse danger. If a child goes dolally, you embrace him to hold in his limbs and stop him from being aggressive. It's a gesture of love as well as of control. We saw the US military as an out-of-control child. Not necessarily bad, but capable of doing bad things. The idea of encircling the base with women was an assertion of power through numbers, of closing the entrances to the base and containing it without hurting those who worked there. This was important to us—our choice in working for peace was non-violence.

Weaving is another theme common to witches and the peace movement.

The idea of weaving the web came from the American peace movement. The year before Greenham, there was an action against the Pentagon when by weaving yarn, women sealed up its entrances. We were consciously reclaiming the tools women were allowed in pre-Industrial and early industrial periods: spinning and working at looms. We also called on the symbolism of the spider and the web. Women have always lived in harmony with the spider: it helps to clean the home by consuming bugs. The notion of the spider's web—building something strong from strands that are individually fragile—was important. We can't do much as individuals, but once we are connected, we are powerful. The interconnectedness of the web with its diffuse lines of communication offers a means of getting away from the linear approach of male politics; it shows that there are many routes to an end point and we probably need them all.

Did you consciously engage with pagan ceremony?

I was very frightened before my first action—I'd never broken the law before, and I was about to invade a nuclear base. We formed a circle, holding hands, each of us focusing on what we would do, the steps we would take and how we would succeed safely and maintaining non-violence, then one of the women starting keening: she set up a note and fluctuated it. I joined in and each of us took a note. As I did so, I felt a huge strength, calmness and confidence descend on me. Confidence in all the other women and in myself. It was tangible. At the end, one of the Welsh activists gave us each a piece of thyme to rub in our palms and put in our pockets "to make sure you have enough time". Magic doesn't work that directly; thyme doesn't give you time, but it summoned up an idea. The action went brilliantly. We hardly knew each other, but we worked in harmony, and in my time at Greenham I came to trust that things would go well if we did this calming or summoning ceremony. Years later I read Starhawk, the pagan author and activist, and discovered that the very things we did are techniques of Wicca.

You wrote a song about witches that has become an anthem in the peace movement, with the chorus, "We are the witches who will never be burned, We are the witches who have learned what it is to be free."

I sang the witches' song from Greenham to the Women in Black in Belgrade and it became almost an anthem for them—it's a lovely chorus to sing in any language. The Women in Black seem to have developed independently of us to challenge militarism, and drew on a deep seam of witch lore in that region. In some parts of the Balkans, villages lost 30 or 40 per cent of their women at one sweep during the witch trials. I was amazed when I found that one of their logos was a witch on a broomstick; they wore it on t-shirts with a slogan underneath in Serbian which translated as "Always disobedient".

"Now Isis was a woman who possessed words of power… And she meditated in her heart, saying, 'Cannot I by means of the sacred name of God make myself mistress of the Earth and become a goddess…?'"

***THE BOOK OF THE DEAD*, E. A. WALLIS BUDGE**

Goddess of secret words

Isis, queen of ancient Egypt's gods, is mistress of the words of power. Only she knows the secret pronunciation, tone of voice, gestures and timing that compel all living things to stop, listen and do as she bids. Such words has she at the tip of her tongue and such incantations that the great god Ra gives up his hidden name to her, which must only be revealed at the point of death. She also has healing language at her disposal; after Ra admits his name, she soothes him with emollient words (she can be called on for intercession by all who heal the sick).

Isis is a mother goddess, called Lady of Life or Green Goddess, and depictions of her suckling her infant son-god have been compared to those of Mary, mother of Jesus. Another of her titles is Maker of the Sunrise. But like all mother goddesses. Isis also holds sway over the world of death and decay. If you know her words of power, you can gain her protection in the underworld; it's worth it, because she has the power to halt or even reverse decay after death. In some incarnations Isis has wings and with these and her precise utterances fans into her beloved husband Osiris just enough life after his death to conceive a son, the god Horus. Witches have always been thought to have the power to take a man's semen without his knowing. Finally, Isis is one more witch trope—the Godmother is another of her titles.

left: *Isis Feeding Horus*, Date unknown, Egyptian

Isis wears a headdress made from the horns of a cow cradling a Sun disc. But like the diadems of so many goddesses, it also resembles crescent Moons.

Spell books

A witch or wise woman's written store of spells resembled a compilation of recipes and may have passed from generation to generation like well-thumbed and stained "receipts" for favourite family dishes. A housewife's treasured recipe book has always contained instructions for non-culinary enterprises: in previous centuries, they would include facial toners, charms for warts, tips on making syrups and cordials, cleaning lore and herbal remedies for minor ailments. A typical book compiled in England between 1700 and 1739 by Mrs Kathleen Palmer is entitled, A Collection of ye best Receipts…in Cookery, preserving, and all manner of Housewifery, physick & Chirurgery. The tradition continued late into the 20th century in collections published by the Women's Institute in the UK, and is echoed in current books of housekeeping tips, especially the 1001 variety. This is information the good housewife of every era is expected to master.

What made spell books distinct? They threw into the mix borrowed religious rites, prayer forms, liturgical language and astrological symbolism. In Russia, a spell commonly began by invoking the power of a saint before setting out the practical instructions: what to do when, and where to begin the spell. Then more religious content was added, such as an extract from the New Testament or the life of a saint in which Christ or the saint encountered and overcame a difficulty similar (physically or symbolically) to the spell-maker's trouble (scenes with rocks and serpents seem common).

After more practical details had been established, such as how the trouble would disappear (instruc-tions might include burying something that would rot, along with the trouble), a locking-in phrase would seal the intention and the magic, often, the last line of a prayer, particularly the Lord's Prayer.

Writing down a magic formula fixed its form, making it specific to the person who possessed the book. This form of copyrighting might be sealed with a warning to users that communicating the spell would nullify its potency. However, from the 18th century, numerous chapbook editions of spellbooks and *grimoires* were published in Germany, Scandinavia and above all France, finally setting out the secrets of herbs, stones, stars, dreams, words and numbers for all who could read.

following page: ***Country Housewife and Lady's Director in the Management of the House*, R. Bradley, 1736, British**

Title page to one of the first cook books.

Sturt Sc.

THE

Country Housewife

AND

LADY's DIRECTOR,

IN THE

Management of a HOUSE, and the Delights and Profits of a FARM.

CONTAINING

INSTRUCTIONS for managing the Brew-House, and Malt-Liquors in the Cellar; the making of Wines of all sorts.

DIRECTIONS for the DAIRY, in the Improvement of Butter and Cheese upon the worst of Soils; the feeding and making of Brawn; the ordering of Fish, Fowl, Herbs, Roots, and all other useful Branches belonging to a Country-Seat, in the most elegant manner for the Table.

Practical OBSERVATIONS concerning DISTILLING; with the best Method of making Ketchup, and many other curious and durable Sauces.

The whole distributed in their proper MONTHS, from the Beginning to the End of the Year.

With particular REMARKS relating to the Drying or Kilning of SAFFRON.

By R. BRADLEY,
Professor of Botany in the University of Cambridge, *and* F. R. S.

The Sixth Edition.
With ADDITIONS.

LONDON:
Printed for D. BROWNE, at the *Black-Swan* without *Temple-Bar*.
MDCCXXXVI. 1736
[Price 2*s.* 6*d.*]

Mother Ivey's curse

**"I curse thee with a great curse,
The sweepings of the gutters of the city be thy food,
The drains of the city be thy drink,
The shadow of the wall be thy abode,
The thresholds be thy dwelling place;
Drunkard and sot strike thy cheek!"**

***DESCENT OF THE GODDESS ISHTAR INTO THE LOWER WORLD*, IN *THE CIVILIZATION OF BABYLONIA AND ASSYRIA*, M. JASTROW**

There is a field overlooking the Atlantic Ocean that remains fallow to this day thanks to the curses of a 16th-century witch. In centuries past, the Hellyer family of Harlyn Bay in Cornwall had a lucrative business catching, salting and packing pilchards, then shipping them by the barrel to Italy. The starving villagers they employed were too poor to eat the fish they risked their lives harvesting, and the motto carved into the granite lintel of the fish cellars they worked in was cruelly ironic—*Dulcis Lucri Odor*, "profit smells sweet". Its warning is legible still.

One day, a large cargo of pilchards was returned from Italy unsold. Though past their best, the fish would have been a blessing for the poverty-stricken villagers. Mother Ivey, a local wise woman, approached the Hellyers, requesting that the fish be donated to ease their suffering. Her request was denied and the pilchards ploughed into a field as fertilizer. In her wrath, Mother Ivey cursed the field, proclaiming that if ever its soil were broken, death would follow. The family continued to use the field until shortly after, when the eldest son, riding over that field, was thrown from his horse and died. For fear of the curse striking again, the land was left fallow for centuries, and the tale survived as a Hellyer family legend, passed from father to son. During World War II, the Hellyers convinced the Agricultural Committee to leave the field fallow despite the "dig for victory" campaign, but the Home Guard insisted on digging defensive trenches there. Within days, the eldest Hellyer son met a grisly end. Ownership of the estate eventually passed on and the new owners, desperate to cleanse the land of its curse, enlisted the help of a local wise woman or "peller", ("repeller" or "expeller"), who recited incantations over a tin stuffed with fabric before burying it in the field. In the 1970s, a group of metal detector enthusiasts began digging in the field, unaware of its deadly history. Within days, one of their number suffered a fatal heart attack. In the 1990s, despite fervent warnings from local people, a water company disturbed the soil to lay pipes. The following day the foreman lay dead also. The farmhouse itself, an imposing grey presence, revealed an equally ghastly history: 20th-century renovation work revealed hidden staircases and rooms showing evidence of torture. To this day the cursed field remains fallow and Mother Ivey's presence still lingers there.

Chimes, rhymes and jingles

It's no coincidence that in the 1833 edition of her book of *Melodies*, old Mother Goose describes her collection of ditties as "enchanting". Who is this old woman who weaves words that spellbind a "parcel of children" but a witch? Each of her "spells", or nursery rhymes, is a short, often nonsensical, jingle or incantation, that, like many charms, has best effect when repeated out loud in company. Through chanting, her young charges memorize her words, which, says Mother Goose, annoys parents, who would prefer that their infants were introduced to "nice catechisms, primers, hymn books and so". Or the national curriculum, for nursery staff today take on Mother Goose's persona when they teach her rhymes to groups of children.

The nursery verses responsible for introducing generations to characters such as Little Boy Blue, Little Miss Muffet and Baby Bunting first appeared in print in England around 1765, and in America within 30 years, but they may have hatched in France.

In the mid-17th-century, *a conte de la mere l'oye* referred to a nonsense tale told by chattering old gossips. It had ribald associations. Geese were associated with suggestive bottom waving, feather beds, prostitution and the storks that bring children (and enjoy springtime frolics)—no surprise that Mother Goose turns up today in pantomime drag. The verses Ma'am Goose tells have some equally suggestive sources, including bawdy broadsides and popular ballads. But, like the spells of the early modern witch, their rag-bag of borrowed, stolen and inherited word sounds also include the riddle, skipping, counting and finger-play games, dances, folk songs and lullabies.

Despite her title, this bird woman in a granny's bonnet and

spectacles has no children of her own. Yet she's an über-mother, always trailed by a bunch of adoring children (or goslings) who she gathers to her petticoats. And the switch side of an adoring mother, suggest fairy tales and child psychologists alike, is a witch. Mother Goose's first popular depiction by the wood engraver Nathaniel Dearborn, who was working around the American city of Boston, shows her as a crone with a hooked nose and upward-pointing chin that make her head resemble a crescent Moon. The Germanic goddess Hulda mines similar territory, being simultaneously goddess of the underworld and protector of the spirits of children. Hulda's alter-ego Frau Holle spins flax as addictively as Mother Goose spins tales (the old mother has appeared with a spindle since her first publishing outing) and flies through the night sky on a goose.

"Ride a cock horse to Banbury Cross,
To see an old woman jump on a black horse."

MOTHER GOOSE RHYME

following page: ***Mother Goose Melodies*, Nathaniel Dearborn, 1833, American**

Like the goddess Isis, who spun spell-binding words with healing powers, Mother Goose has always used words to keep children "quiet when they were in pain". This is the frontispiece from the 1833 edition of *Mother Goose's Melodies*.

THE ONLY
TRUE
MOTHER GOOSE.
BOSTON:
MUNROE & FRANCIS.

“Hear what ma’am goose says!

My dear little Blossoms, there are now in this world, and always will be, a great many grannies beside myself, both in petticoats and pantaloons, some a deal younger to be sure; but all monstrous wise, and of my own family name. These old women, who never had chick nor child of their own, but who always know how to bring up other people’s children, will tell you with very long faces, that my enchanting, quieting, soothing volume, my all-sufficient anodyne for cross, peevish, won’t-be-comforted little bairns, ought to be laid aside for more learned books, such as they could select and publish. Fudge! I tell you that all their batterings can’t deface my beauties, nor their wise pratings equal my wiser prattlings; and all imitators of my refreshing songs might as well write a new Billy Shakespeare as another Mother Goose: we two great poets were born together, and we shall go out of the world together

No, no, my Melodies will never die,
While nurses sing, or babies cry.”

Spinning a yarn

Witches are traditionally thought of as spinsters: literally, women who spin, but also solitary women past the age of child-bearing. Spinning seems associated with a loss of female hormones—in Mexico it is said that in pre-Conquest times, mothers threatened their daughters that if they did not learn to spin, they would become men. The poet Penelope Shuttle suggests that the spinster might be so named because she has spun thorough the months—menstruating each month rather than taking a break for pregnancy or nursing.

A woman who spins (or weaves) guides something from nothing to great complexity, and has the power to forge endless potential forms. So potent is this art that it is likened to the act of creating life, as magical as the journey from single cell to safely birthed baby—and equally fraught with potential danger. In Roman mythology, the Parcae carry spindles on which they tease out men's lives and choose when to snap the thread. In many places, spindles and spinning wheels were traditionally made from rowan wood, the witch tree, which confers protection from enchantment.

When women gathered together to spin or weave, they might also weave stories to ease the boredom of the mundane, repetitive tasks; in Italy the stock phrase for beginning tales of wonder is not "once upon a time", but *Nel tempo over Bertha filava*; "the days when Bertha spun". Bertha is a folk name that to the Grimms denoted grandmother or female ancestors, and might be related to Berchta, the monstress-spinner who oversees the quality of women's work. In the form of the Austrian-German Perchta, cousin of La Befana, she circulates at Christmas with gifts for the good. But instead of filling the stockings of the bad, she slits their stomachs open and fills them with garbage.

As old wives pass on their fantastical stories of other worlds, embroidering the detail and stock patterns to make them their own, might they not also, worried medieval theologians, pass on secret or forbidden knowledge that could threaten social and temporal order? Might she not weave plots within her plots; for the tales she told were of transgression—people are not whom they seem, and social states can be waved aside by magic or disguise. Might talk of shape-shifting weave ill-fortune, disruption and spirits into the material world? Or fill those who heard them with garbage? Spindles were potential weapons of treachery. In 14th-century depictions of witches from northern Europe, they aim their pointed spindles like revolvers to ward off wild beasts. One hundred years later, it was commonly hinted that women used their long stiff "weapons" in orgiastic night-time rites.

Women, too, invested in the dangers inherent in spinning, developing protective rituals to police the act. They might weave protective motifs into the final piece of fabric, such as choppy boundary lines or a single red thread, and engage in rituals to protect the equipment after work finished and overnight, or on holy days. To Slavic peoples, Friday (the Goddess's day) is a day of rest, and a protective but vindictive witch spirit, Mother Friday, stalks the evenings to ensure that the sabbath is honoured and that women are not sewing, spinning or weaving, acts that cause her eyes to silt up with dust.

following page: **Detail from *Spinning the Web of Fate*, Hans Weiditz, 1532, German**

In this woodcut a witch holds a spindle in one hand and in the other several spindles attached to a broom. With them, she weaves the magic of the Moon and the stars into the warp and weft of our world.

"Have you been present at, or consented to, the vanities which women practice in their woollen work, in their weaving, who, when they begin their weaving, hope to be able to bring it about that with incantations and with their own actions that the threads of the warp and the woof become so intertwined that unless someone makes use of their other diabolical counter-incantations he will perish totally?"

***CORRECTOR*, BURCHARD OF WORMS**

Mother Friday

There was once a certain woman who did not pay due reverence to Mother Friday, but set to work on a distaff full of flax, combing it and whirling it. She spun away until dinner-time, then sleep fell upon her, Suddenly the door opened, and in came Mother Friday, before the eyes of all who were there, clad in a white dress, and in such a rage! And she went straight up to the woman who had been spinning, and scooped up from the floor a handful of the dust that had fallen out of the flax, and began stuffing and stuffing that woman's eyes full of it! After she had stuffed them full, she went off in a rage, disappeared without saying a word.

When the woman awoke, she began squalling, at the top of her voice, about her eyes, but could not tell what was the matter with them. The other women, who had been much frightened, began to cry out: "Oh, you wretch, you! You've brought a terrible punishment on yourself from Mother Friday." Then they told her all that had taken place. She listened to it all, and then began imploring: "Mother Friday, forgive me! Pardon me, the guilty one! I'll offer thee a taper, and I'll never let friend or foe dishonour thee, Mother!"

Well what do you think? During the night, back came Mother Friday, and took the dust out of that woman's eyes, so that she was able to get about again. It's a great sin to dishonour Mother Friday, combing and spinning flax, forsooth!

THE MAGIC OF THE HORSE-SHOE, **ROBERT MEANS LAWRENCE**

Story-telling

Telling tales is a form of magic—conjuring characters and scenes from thin air; transporting an audience to far-off lands and into other bodies; uttering magic formula like "once upon a time" and "happily ever after". The spinster who weaves stories of witches and fairies and Mother Goose, the old bawd who delights infants with riddles and cautionary tales, might be compared to the magician-bards of Celtic tradition. They curated, carried and transmitted down the generations the accumulated knowledge that defined tribal identity: genealogy and history, language and laws, spiritual wisdom and the stories of iconic heroes. While chronicling life as it rolled out, they were also holders of the future. They were "seers" (the term for a bard in Ireland and Scotland, *filidh*, derives from a root meaning "to see"), with the gift of future-sight. So highly regarded were the bards that they were considered beyond the law. They were fearless satirists who could destroy reputations and with their well-wrought curses were said to bring about illness or worse. In order to become such a revered and feared figure, an Irish bard would undergo a lengthy formal apprenticeship, not only in music and poetic metre, story "shells", history and culture, but in more magical arts: secret alphabets, science, alchemy and astronomy. They would choose a bardic name that expressed their nature and prophesied the person they would evolve into, just as Wiccans do today. This poetic name could also serve as a spell or incantation that would allow them to shift in shape and through time.

following page: ***The Storyteller*, Lorenz Frolich, 1850–1875, Danish**

Captivated children listen to a young story-teller. Theirs is a secret world where anything is possible because adults are excluded.

Mother of a seer

Taleisin, Wales's finest bard, was a professional poet who, in the latter part of the 6th century, served as bard in the court of at least three Welsh princes. Some say he served King Arthur, too, for Taliesin is also a mythological being who flows through time and shifts in shape. Taliesin's name, meaning "Radiant Brow", hints at his supernatural and prophetic capabilities. At the brow sits the third eye, which, once opened, is believed in Hinduism and Buddhism to confer the ability to see beyond time: to judge the past, draw conclusions from the present and foresee what is to come. This is the wisdom of enlightenment. As well as foresight, Taleisin has the power to stir up winds and control the behaviour of cattle and horses. If these recall the gifts of witches, it's because they are. He obtained them from his mother, the enchantress Ceridwen, goddess of poetry and the source of divine inspiration.

Ceridwen had a daughter, the fairest in the world, and a son, as ugly and weak-witted as his sister was fair. And so to give her son the opportunity to enter the company of noblemen, she does what every mother aspires to; she drags out her magic cauldron of inspiration and starts to brew some mead that will confer on whoever drinks it the mysteries of knowledge and inspiration. After a lengthy and exhausting search for the exact herbs, she allows the brew to simmer for a year and a day, reducing to three drops of inspiration (the rest is poison). But these three drops of "charmed liquor" fall onto the hand of the servant boy Gwion Bach, who tries to cool his hand by sucking it. Thus he gains the power of vision and inspiration intended for Ceridwen's boy-child. Foreseeing the future, Gwion Bach flees the witch's house, revealing his new powers of transformation as he swiftly shape-shifts from rabbit to fish to bird to corn. The witch echoes his transformations each time, becoming dog to his rabbit, river to his fish, hawk to his bird and hen to his grain of corn, gobbling him up. She becomes pregnant with the grain and eventually gives birth to an infant so radiant that she knows at first sight that he is an enlightened being. Unable to kill him, as planned, the enchantress thrusts the baby into a leather bag and casts him into the ocean. The child is found by a prince out fishing for salmon, the fish of great wisdom. On pulling the infant from the water, the prince cries out "*Taliesin*", Radiant Brow. The infant immediately spouts sublime verse telling the prince that their meeting is predestined, and soon after is performing magic and composing epic poetry at the courts of kings.

"And she went forth after him, running. And he saw her, and changed himself into a hare and fled. But she changed herself into a greyhound and turned him. And he ran towards a river, and became a fish. And she in the form of an otter-bitch chased him under the water, until he was fain to turn himself into a bird of the air. She, as a hawk, followed him and gave him no rest in the sky. And just as she was about to stoop upon him, and he was in fear of death, he espied a heap of winnowed wheat on the floor of a barn, and he dropped among the wheat, and turned himself into one of the grains. Then she transformed herself into a high-crested black hen, and went to the wheat and scratched it with her feet, and found him out and swallowed him."

***THE MABINOGION*, TRANSLATED BY LADY CHARLOTTE GUEST**

Witch to priest

Interview with Rev. Graham Taylor

Hailed as "the new C. S. Lewis", G. P. Taylor is former parish priest of Cloughton in North Yorkshire and St. Mary's in Whitby, the site of Dracula's grave in Bram Stoker's novel. He is author of the bestselling children's fantasy novel *Shadowmancer*, a dark thriller about witchcraft with clear Christian themes, which topped the New York Times bestseller list and spent 15 weeks at the top of the British book charts. Subsequent novels include *Wormwood*, *Tersias*, *The Curse of Salamander Street* and *Mariah Mundi: the Midas Box*; G. P. Taylor has also presented the ITV programme about the paranormal, *Uninvited Guests*. *Shadowmancer* has been translated into 48 languages and has sold more than four and a half million copies worldwide; it is due to be filmed by Plymouth Rock Studios.

As a Christian, why did you set your novel in a world of witchcraft?

I was a practising witch! I got into it after a near-death experience at the age of six when I fell into a river, drowned and was resuscitated. Growing up on a council estate, my parents weren't interested in spirituality, and for years I didn't know where to go to discuss my experience and my anxiety about what happens when we die. I was interested in meditation for a while; I looked into Christianity, which I found lacking, and into Islam. Then, in my teens, I met a man in the witchcraft section of the local library and he invited me to his occult shop; basically he was a bit of a weirdo, but it was there that I started to practise magic. I explored Crowellian and Gardnerian witchcraft among other forms, but when I eventually looked into the theology, there was nothing there; just bad poetry. I discovered that witchcraft didn't come from an ancient tradition; it was made up in modern times. There was no early modern witchcraft either: that was just an idea devised by the church to subjugate women. I know lots of witches and they're very nice; it's a great way of exploring yourself if that's what rocks your boat. The only real witch in *Shadowmancer* is benevolent. The evil figure is a magician; in my experience these men tend to be sex crazed and power mad.

previous page: **Rev. G. P. Taylor, www.sarahphotgirl.com, 2006, British**

Did you take any aspects of Wicca with you when you became a Church of England priest?

I always loved the relationship witchcraft has with the Earth—the seasons, the Sun and the Moon. When I was priest in Ravenscar, I invented a "heather service"; we would go out onto the moors and cut heather, bless it and then give it out for people to take into hospital. We were taking God's goodness—the curative powers of the moorland—indoors to help heal the sick. There's a great deal of our pagan past in the Bible, and Jesus was very much in touch with the pattern of the seasons. In the church we need to tie ourselves in more with the physicality of the seasons—the fruit of summer, the renewal of spring, the darkness of winter. I like the way that the time of the oak in paganism gives way to the time of the holly; people need that mystery in their lives.

Witchcraft is the fastest-growing faith system among teenagers in the UK. How do you explain this?

People love it; they want something extra in their lives and occult practices let them have a faith without subscribing to anything outside themselves. And Wicca allows girls to get in touch with feminine power; occultism celebrates women and in many covens the female is considered higher than the male. The Church of England is far too masculine; it lacks a focus on spiritual wisdom, which is always referred to as feminine in the Greek-–the misogynists in the early church reigned in that side of Christianity; can't have women in positions of power, can we? We need to be more down to earth spiritually in the church; to root ourselves in the world and centre people in who they are in God, so that Christianity is cake on the plate while we wait not just a treat after we die.

You've said that people who explore the occult invite spirits into their homes, and that, for you, this has led to an increase in requests for exorcisms.

I've found that ghosts fall into four categories: residual memories played back, like a hologram that fades over the years; poltergeists who feed on a source of power; and spirits of the dear departed who haven't yet realized they are dead. Then there are negative evil forces, but I hardly ever come across these. What's most common is the type of call I got recently from a young professional couple in an old house. When I got there, I couldn't feel a thing. The woman had been involved in spiritualism and tarot cards, and loved horror films. She was so turned on to this way of thinking that she'd projected all this stuff. People so love to be terrified that they're looking for triggers for their fears. She showed me some dried flowers which had been mysteriously scattered over the floor. All I saw was a vase that had tipped over. I hummed a bit and prayed for their child; that was all they needed; reassurance. It was the same during the feng-shui craze a few years ago; all people seek is reassurance. But I once spooked some teenagers who were causing disturbances in the village churchyard at night; I put on my white hooded robe and appeared among the gravestones. That got rid of them....

The charmed pot

Not seen in the iconography of witches before 1489, the cauldron had become an emblem of witchcraft by the 16th century, perhaps thanks to influential translations of classical poetry that described sorceresses such as Medea brewing magic potions in great pots. Ever since, the cauldron has become a byword for mystical female powers or glamour, It is a womb-shaped container where warmth and moisture transform raw ingredients into much more than the sum of their parts. Modern witches use it in rituals as a representation of the feminine principle and the elements water and fire as well as practically, to mix herbs and essences.

Irish tales tell of a great cauldron in the underworld with the power to heal the wounded and bring the dead back to life. For this reason, it is associated with great wisdom, including the secret knowledge of other worlds. Many Wiccan information sites offering advice, information and spiritual succour take on this role today, along with its name.

The cauldron is also the great family cooking pot: the cast-iron casserole or copper preserving pan happily bubbling at the heart of the home, the hearth. Like the cauldron of the great Irish god of good, Daghda, which never empties, mother's pot represents contentment. Many of the symbols associated with witches are indistinguishable from the tools that a woman uses to make a happy home, and so become profoundly disturbing if used not to nurture but to harm.

"Double, double toil and trouble;
Fire, burn; and cauldron, bubble."

MACBETH, WILLIAM SHAKESPEARE

Angelic potions

Christian writings from the second-century BCE, (Enoch I) describes how a band of rebel angels descends to Earth and "defile themselves" with human women, after which, they kindly teach them the ways of plants and roots, charms and enchantments. In effect, these angels create the first witches, define them as healers as much as magic-makers, and suggest that all women might share in the powers. The art of curing with herbs and store-cupboard ingredients was expected of the housewife in eras when doctors and apothecaries were scarce and expensive. Anyone who was especially skilled in it might gain such a reputation for her healing prowess that others would come to her for advice, remedies, or simply a blessing. So acclaimed were wise women healers that the great 14th-century Swiss physician Paracelsus claimed that physicians could learn much from them.

There was no clear-cut distinction between magic and medicine in the early modern era. Indeed, magic healers and physicians worked from the same texts, such as Nicholas Culpeper's *The English Physician or Herball* (1653). Some commentators note that wise-women healers may have achieved better results than men of medicine because they took a holistic approach, considering not just the body, but the spirit.

previous page: ***Witches Standing at Cauldron*, Artist unknown, *c.*1500, German**

Woodcut from around 1500 used to illustrate a book by Professor Ulrich Molitor which was designed to remove doubts about the existence of witchcraft. The witches tending to a cauldron are brewing a storm with ingredients including a cockerel and a snake.

Cures were sought for ailments with physical cause and for ills wrought by witchcraft. Indeed, little distinction was made between the two—if you don't understand how illness arises, its origins might as well be supernatural as physiological. Believing in the power of charms and sympathetic acts—like using a ritual pitchfork to toss away troubles—gave sufferers a sense of control over life's arbitrary forces.

Stock herbal charms against bewitching tended to be based upon St. John's wort, vervain and dill. These herbs are effective against stress, infections and "female" complaints, so may have been well suited to a wise woman's clients. Fear of bewitchment (and of being labelled a witch) could cause such extreme stress, posit some modern commentators, that they could trigger physical and mental symptoms. Today, St. John's wort is used to treat tension, anxiety, insomnia and depression, and is considered useful for viral infections and for its anti-inflammatory and antiseptic properties. Vervain is a cure-all, used for headaches, digestive problems, asthma, flu and PMT, and is helpful in labour and nursing. It works on the parasympathetic nervous system, and is especially useful for nervous tension and depression and for those convalescing. Dill derives from the Norse word *dylla*, meaning "to soothe", and is used for digestive complaints, menstrual and nursing difficulties. Wise women were known for their prowess in treating symptoms of the pre- and post-natal periods, times when the body is prone to complications (including those brought about by the malicious work of witches). Difficulties with breastfeeding were often blamed on witches, and could result in the death of a child in the era before formula milk, so being able to treat such problems would be especially important for the wise woman.

“divers honest persons, as well men as women,…God hath endowed with the knowledge of the nature kind and operation of certain herbs, roots and waters, and the using and ministering to them to such as be pained with customable disease.”

ACT OF ENGLISH PARLIAMENT, 1542

left: ***The Archbishop Watches Elise in the Churchyard*, Helen Stratton, *c.*1900, British**

Elise gathers herbs in the churchyard watched over by the archbishop, who believes her to be a witch. With the nettles Elise will weave shirts to release her 11 brothers who were transformed into wild swans by a wicked queen. She learned the secret of the plants from an old woman she met in the forest, who is the sorceress Morgana.

Harmful magic

**"Mind the Threefold Law you should,
Three times bad and three times good."**

FROM THE *WICCAN CREDO* (*c.*1910 OR 1940S/50S)

Maleficium is the intentional practice of sorcery for harm (most often to people, animals or crops) and it made up the bulk of accusations of witchcraft in the early modern era. When ordinary people suffered misfortune, they looked for a reason and for a few hundred years found it in witches.

Witches were said to be capable of harming by calling up destructive forces in nature (storms and pestilence) and within men and women (anger, greed and the urge for revenge) and by using other-worldly means to influence our world. This, they did by performing rites using magic symbols, numbers and words (speaking or writing charms or names backward was thought to be effective). The church spread the word that witches did their evil deeds after agreeing a pact with the devil or his demons.

Hexing is strictly prohibited among modern witches, who tend to live by the Wiccan Rede (the latter word derives from the Old Enlgish *roedan*, "to guide or direct"). This states that we are free to do whatever we wish, as long as it harms nobody, including ourselves. "Harming" in this case is understood to encompass actively causing physical injury and trying to influence someone's opinion. The guidance of the Rede is underpinned by the Threefold Law, the belief that whatever we do, whether for good or ill, comes back to us three times over. Cleansing spells are encouraged as a means of ridding physical spaces of ill-intentioned energies, and to rid oneself of negative emotions, such as envy or anger. Words and rites may also be used to remove the mental, emotional and psychic blocks to compassion and self-realization. Today, one would probably see a counsellor to deal with the destructive emotions that witches formerly dealt in, such as lust and revenge.

above: Illustrations of hex symbols; these geometric folk-art designs based on stars, rosettes, Sun and Moon shapes inscribed within a circle were painted on furniture and household objects by German-speaking settlers in Pennsylvania from the 17th-century, and later enlarged to paint on barns, either to ward off evil or as a good-fortune charm.

following page: **Detail from *Tontlawald Feeds a Snake*, H. J. Ford, 1907, British**

A girl desperate to escape her wicked stepmother flees to an "other" world, the Tontlawald, in an Estonian tale. Here, the supernatural folk shape a clay doll to take her place in the real world: no matter how hard the stepmother beats the clay child, she feels no pain. The doll is animated by a drop of the girl's blood, stuck into its heart with a golden needle, and by a snake, which kills the wicked mother.

Poppets

In her trial testimony, published in 1612, the Pendle Witch Elizabeth Sowtherns describes the "speediest" way to take a man's life by witchcraft. First make a "Picture of Clay", shaped like the victim and dry it thoroughly. Then, when you "would have them to be ill in any one place more than an other", take a thorn or pin and prick that part of the "Picture". To have any part of the body "consume away", burn that piece. To destroy the entire body, take "the remnant of the sayd Picture, and burne it".

These small figurines, which could also be of wax or clay, were known as poppets, and a famous example sat at the centre of a royal witchcraft plot in London in 1578, when three wax figures were found impaled with hog's bristle. The middle one had the name of Queen, Elizabeth inscribed upon it. In trial reports, poppets sometimes seem interchangeable in name with a witch's familiar spirits. Interestingly, the word is a term of endearment for a small child, especially if ill or out of sorts, and a poppet may also be called a *mamet* (a breast-fed infant). Like the familiar, the poppet may have been thought of as a witch's strange child, and in some traditions they were used as a fertility charm for the bed of newlyweds

In the Russian tradition, dolls or moppets were thought to be the final resting place of spirits, which, if vindictive, could upset a happy family home (the theme is continued in numerous modern horror films). But in fairy tales, such as "Beautiful Vasilisa", the doll is inhabited by the spirit of a nurturing mother figure, who empowers the girl with all the skills and confidence she needs to stand up to the terrifying witch Baba Yaga.

The magic bargain

"On one condition" says the fairy-tale crone when the protagonist crosses her path asking for a favour, for she is queen of the magical test. She might be encountered in her own form, as a crone, or in disguise, perhaps as a beggarwoman or a fine lady, but in each case sets a near-impossible task; the outcome rests on the moral character of the protagonist. If she shows ingenuity, industriousness, bravery and a generous heart, the witch rewards her well. But those who try to cheat the witch's test or who are not good at heart are cursed.

In the Grimm Brothers' story "Mother Holle" (*aka* "Mother Holda"), the golden girl who does the housework impeccably is rewarded with "boiled or roast meat every day" and a shower of gold. The witch showers a kettle of pitch over the lazy girl who acts surly, and "it could not be removed as long as she lived".

In the Perrault tale "Diamonds and Toads", a sweet-natured, beautiful and hardworking girl meets "a poor woman who begged" in the forest, and helps this "good wife" to a drink. Bingo! Now whenever the girl speaks, flowers and jewels spill from her mouth. Her half-sister, an "ill-bred minx", grumbles all the way to the forest carrying a cup, instructed by her mother to bring home more treasure. The "proud saucy one" meets not a beggarwoman but a lady "most gloriously dressed", to whom she rages, "Am I come hither to serve you with water pray? I suppose the silver tankard was brought purely for your ladyship, was it?" For her lack of breeding, the witch curses the "pert hussy" to utter only snakes and toads. The moral? Act kindly to odd old ladies who cross your path. They have the power to hex you (in German tales such characters are referred to as witches) or to protect you and use their decades of experience to develop your potential (in French tales they are fairy godmothers).

Cinderella has the best-known godmother of all. So sure is she of the child's innate goodness that she acts in *loco parentis*, preparing Cinders to enter the world of courting and status (her birthright as a gentleman's daughter), and making sure she stays safe by coming home before midnight. Traditionally, the godmother played an intimate role in family life, assisting a mother in child birth and during the post-natal period before helping mother and baby to the churching. Being with the baby before and during birth brought her a deep knowledge of the infant's character and family values, and ensured that she could be trusted to take some responsibility for the child. These are the riches the fairy godmother can confer. However, the role brought the potential for strife, too. Inserting an outsider into the heart of a family can lead to trouble, and women passed over for this important role might feel sore, and be blamed for harm that follows. The godmother (and non-godmother) may curse, too.

following page: ***Cinderella and her Godmother*, Margaret Evans Price, *c.*1920, British**

In illustrations up to the 1960s Cinderella's fairy godmother is depicted wearing a witch's hat, and the first ingredient she asks for to work her transformative magic is a Hallowe'en pumpkin. Cinderella cottons on to the lady's witchy status: when the godmother can't think how to conjure a coachmen, she runs off to find that ever-popular familiar, a rat.

"It is remarkable that nowhere… do the gypsies regard the witch as utterly horrible, diabolical and damnable. She is with them simply a woman who has gained supernatural power, which she uses for good or misuses for evil according to her disposition."

***GYPSY SORCERY AND FORTUNE-TELLING*, CHARLES GODFREY LELAND**

Godmother Magic

Her godmother, who saw her all in tears, asked [Cinderella] what was the matter.

"I wish I could—I wish I could —"; she was not able to speak the rest, being interrupted by her tears and sobbing.

This godmother of hers, who was a fairy, said to her, "Thou wishest thou couldst go to the ball; is it not so?"

"Yes," cried Cinderella, with a great sigh.

"Well," said her godmother, " be but a good girl, and I will contrive that thou shalt go." Then she took her into her chamber, and said to her, "Run into the garden, and bring me a pumpkin."

Cinderella went immediately to gather the finest she could get, and brought it to her godmother, not being able to imagine how this pumpkin could make her go to the ball. Her godmother scooped out all the inside of it, having left nothing but the rind; which done, she struck it with her wand, and the pumpkin was instantly turned into a fine coach, gilded all over with gold.

She then went to look into her mouse-trap, where she found six mice, all alive, and ordered Cinderella to lift up a little the trapdoor, when, giving each mouse, as it went out, a little tap with her wand, the mouse was that moment turned into a fine horse, which altogether made a very fine set of six horses of a beautiful mouse-colored dapple-gray. Being at a loss for a coachman, the godmother could not think of what to use.

"I will go and see," said Cinderella, "if there is never a rat in the rat-trap—we may make a coachman of him."

"Thou art in the right," replied her godmother; "go and look".

Cinderella brought the trap to her, and in it there were three huge rats. The fairy made choice of one of the three which had the largest beard, and, having touched him with her wand, he was turned into a fat, jolly coachman, who had the smartest whiskers eyes ever beheld. After that she said to Cinderella:

"Go again into the garden, and you will find six lizards behind the watering-pot, bring them to me."

She had no sooner done so but her godmother turned them into six footmen, who skipped up immediately behind the coach, with their liveries all bedaubed with gold and silver, and clung as close behind each other as if they had done nothing else their whole lives. The Fairy then said to Cinderella:

"Well, you see here an equipage fit to go to the ball with; are you not pleased with it?"

"Oh! yes," cried she; "but must I go thither as I am, in these nasty rags?"

Her godmother only just touched her with her wand, and, at the same instant, her clothes were turned into cloth of gold and silver, all beset with jewels. This done, she gave her a pair of glass slippers, the prettiest in the whole world. Being thus decked out, she got up into her coach; but her godmother, above all things, commanded her not to stay till after midnight, telling her, at the same time, that if she stayed one moment longer, the coach would be a pumpkin again, her horses mice, her coachman a rat, her footmen lizards, and her clothes become just as they were before.

***CINDERELLA*, *THE BLUE FAIRY BOOK*, CHARLES PERRAULT, ED. ANDREW LANG**

Shape-shifting

Witches don't have stable bodies; at the blink of an eye they can take myriad forms. Witnesses at the trial of Ann Baites, an English woman accused of witchcraft, described seeing her in the shape of a cat, a hare, a hound and a bee, but any creature—domesticated beast, exotic creature or humble bug—can contain a witch's lifeforce. Some mother or nature goddesses are Ladies of the Animals, living so fully with creatures that their bodies seems to mutate into them; hence she can be worshipped in many forms—goddess, bird, fawn or elk. Siberia's mother goddess is also considered creator of shaman, magic mortals who leave their bodies to travel with animal spirits to worlds beyond.

Anyone who transmutes elements from one form to another, such as the blacksmith and the miller, works powerful magic, and is regarded with awe as well as great respect in a community; they become part supernatural being. But changing the form of substances is every woman's work, too. As if by magic, women have always spun base substances (flax, straw, grain) into pure gold (or something worth gold at market). And theirs is the most miraculous transformative act of all: turning semen into a baby. The female body is mutable, of course. It doesn't obey the laws set by the adult male body—our bodies change through the month (our minds and moods, too) and again in the middle of life. So amorphous is this body that it leaks its primal fluids: menstrual blood and mother's milk, which are considered such magical substances that they make their way into spells. When we are attached by an umbilical cord or nurse an infant, the body blurs still more: where does one end and the next begin? Given such formlessness, shape-shifting seems less magical skill than involuntary act.

Because the witch is mutable and leaky, wherever she leaves something of herself, she is vulnerable. If she has soured the milk, a few atoms of witch remain there and thrusting a red-hot poker into the pot will cause her pain. Taking something from the witch—hair, clothing, a pot from her kitchen—also gives power over her. But her blood makes her most vulnerable. If you can catch a witch in human form and penetrate her mortal shell—perhaps by scratching or pricking with a pin—you destroy her powers; all the more if the blood loss is "above the breath": from the veins at her temples. This may be tricky. Because she doesn't obey normal boundary rules, the witch's body, though free-form, seems strangely impermeable—she can even repel bullets and swords.

following page: **Detail from *Tamamo the Fox Maiden*, Warwick Goble, 1910, British**

The Japanese *kitsune* has the power to play with the fabric of life, one moment vixen, the next foxy lady, and she uses it to confound men.

"Strange! Passing strange!
The Death-Stone's rent in twain:
O'er moor and field
A lurid glare
Burns fierce. There stands reavel'd
A fox, and yet again
The phantom seems to wear
The aspect of a maiden fair!

With fervent zeal the great magician prays,
And ev'ry tone with anguish and amaze
O'erpow'rs the witch, who with convulsive grasp
The holy symbols of the gods doth clasp,
And, heav'nward-soaring, flies o'er land and sea
To seek the shelter of this distant lea."

"THE DEATH-STONE", *JAPANESE CLASSICAL POETRY*,
TRANS. BASIL HALL CHAMBERLIN

The familiar

"a thing like a teat, the bigness of the little finger, and the length of half a finger, which was branched at the top like a teat, and seemed as though one had sucked it."

FROM THE TRIAL OF ELIZABETH SAWYER, 1621, REFERRING TO HER WITCHMARK

In some cultures, a totemic guardian spirit, often in the shape of an animal, attaches to a girl at her first period, and her dreams of the creature are considered significant to the community. In early modern England, such encounters were a sure sign that a woman was a witch. Her wicked acts were reported to be directed or performed by "familiars". They resembled a pet crossed with a child's invisible friend, taking the form of cats, mice or rats, moles or toads, but acting like the diminutive domestic sprites of folk and fairy lore such as the brownie, who haunts the hearth and demands tithes. If they didn't have the name of a domesticated animal, they took those of fairies, imps and other supernatural creatures, such as Puck or Robin Goodfellow. In Thomas Middleton's play *The Witch* (c.1609–1616), the creatures we meet stirring the cauldron in the first scene in Hecate's cave include the typically named Titty and Tiffin, Suckin and Pidgen, Liard and Robin. Or familiars might take the fond names used for children; at trial, some witches insisted they were the spirits of her lost children calling and commanding her, or it was said they made cots for them by lining a pot or wicker basket with wool. The play *The Witch of Edmonton* (1621) by William Rowley, Thomas Dekker and John Ford dramatizes the case of Elizabeth Sawyer, hanged for witchcraft in April 1621. Her familiar borrows the form of a spinster's lap dog. They make a rather pathetic couple as she pats her spirit hound saying,

Ho,ho, my dainty,
My little pearl! No lady loves her hound,
Monkey or parakeet, as I do thee.

The spirit abandons her once she is locked in prison. Familiars were said to be nursed on the witch's blood, using a concealed teat. This "witchmark" served as evidence of witchcraft in courts, which employed licensed midwives to search for and diagnose the extra nipple. It was most often discovered in a "dark" place near a woman's "secrets", a sign of the topsy-turvy nature of the nurturing. A woman's body could speak even when she could or would not confess. In a tale from eastern Siberia, a husband only detects that his beautiful wife has been possessed by Yaghishna, grandmother witch (who has dropped the real wife from her soft reindeer skin into an underground cellar "a hundred fathoms deep, a hundred fathoms wide, and quite dark"), when he finds his "wife" suckling their baby son through her left heel.

Matthew Hopkins Witch Finder Gener
My Imps names
Holt
1 Ilemauzar
2 Pyewackett
Jarmara
Sacke
& Sugar
3 Pecke in the Crown
4 Griezzell Greedigu
Newes
Vinegar tom

"...a black thing; it wasn't exactly a dog nor a rat, it looked more like a frog..."

THE IMP BELONGING TO MRS SMITH, A CAMBRIDGESHIRE WITCH

left: ***Matthew Hopkins, Witch Finder General*, Artist unknown, 1792, British**

Print depicting Matthew Hopkins, the 16th-century self-appointed "witch finder", whose freelance work as inquisitor resulted in the investigation of 250 witches in East Anglia, at least 100 of whom were hanged. Detailed accounts of familiars are found in most of the trials with which he was connected. Here, he comes across two witches with their familiars, who range from domestic pet to fantasy animals. The old dames tell us their "imps" names, which include fond terms like Griezzell Greedigutt.

The black cat

"Mrs. Pipchin had an old black cat, who generally lay coiled upon the centre foot of the fender, purring egotistically, and winking at the fire until the contracted pupils of his eyes were like two notes of admiration. The good old lady might have been—not to record it disrespectfully—a witch, and Paul and the cat her two familiars, as they all sat by the fire together. It would have been quite in keeping with the appearance of the party if they had all sprung up the chimney in a high wind one night, and never been heard of any more."

***DOMBEY AND SON*, CHARLES DICKENS**

The black cat is a relatively recent addition to the witch's coterie; not until the 19th century did it take the lead role previously shared by rats, moles and snails—the hare was also called "puss" until the 18th century. The cat became a witch fixture at the same time that cat shows, breeding and pet-pampering took off; previously, cats were domestic rat-catchers. The feline nocturnal habit, aloofness and ability to materialize seemingly from nowhere helped to attach the cat to the witch, as did its supposed powers of divination (cats intuit atmospheric changes, such as storms, before human senses). Early 19th-century "Egyptomania" in Europe may have helped, too. Egypt is famed for domesticating the cat; it is said that the ancient Egyptians valued the way cats' eyes dilate and contract, as if reflecting the phases of the Moon. The goddess Bastet, a relative of the night goddess Neith, was depicted as a woman with a cat's head. A protective goddess, she looked out not only for cats, but for many things feminine (and witchy), including hearth and home, the perfume or ointment jar, and fertility. Like her animal charges and the lunar huntress Artemis/Diana, with whom she became linked later, Bastet was a skilled and instinctive fighter, and the women-only festivities held in her name involved catty name-taunting of women from rival villages. They took place at Hallowe'en and also featured teasing sexual games—the sex kitten has been with us for millennia. Eve, the most teasing temptress of the Biblical witch figures, became associated with the cat early in the Christian era. Despite being declared diabolical by Pope Gregory IX in 1233, black cats are regarded as lucky everywhere but China. In Europe, they are regularly unearthed from beneath the floorboards or windows of old buildings, bricked in to ward off fire, attract husbands for daughters or perhaps to sniff out uncanny prey from other realms.

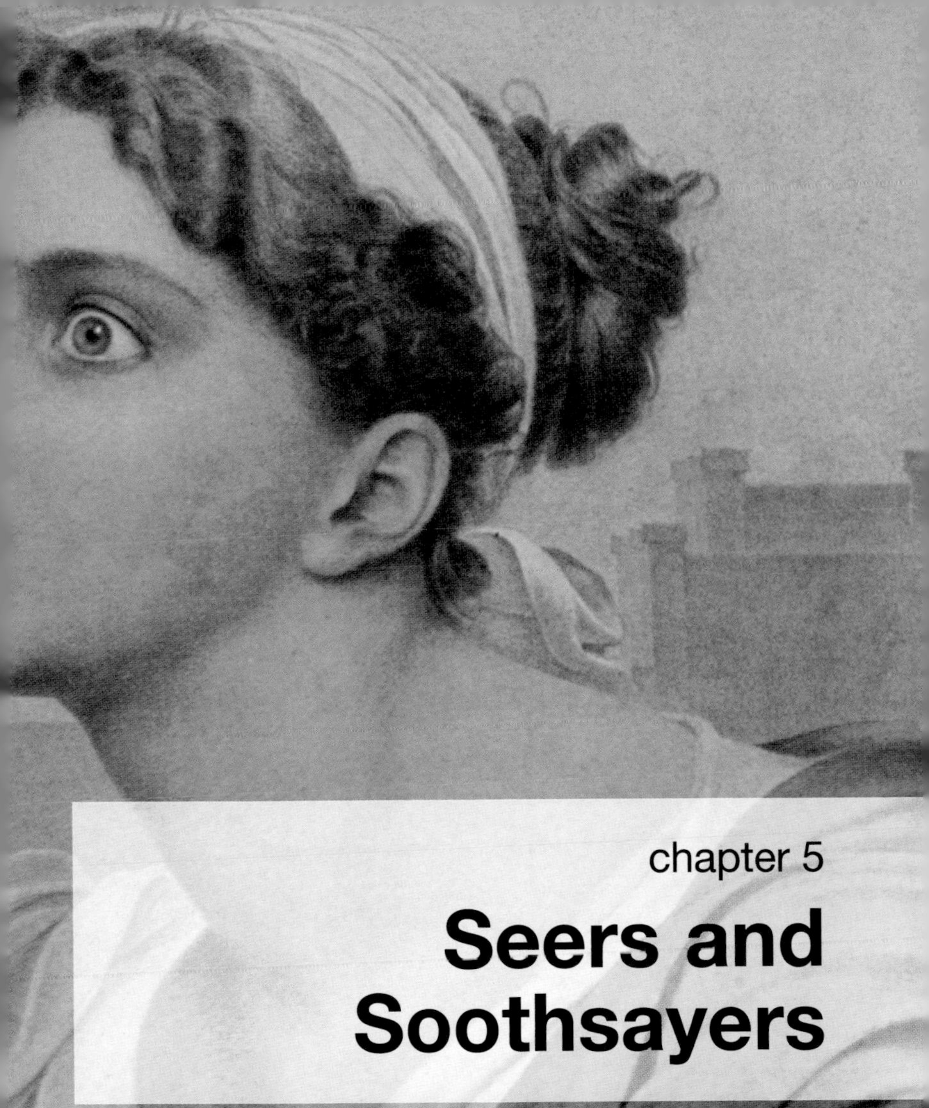

chapter 5

Seers and Soothsayers

News from beyond

"Cassandra cried, and curs'd the unhappy hour;
Foretold our fate; but, by the god's decree,
All heard, and none believ'd the prophecy."

***AENEID*, VIRGIL (29– 19 BCE)**

The clairvoyant or person with second sight is able to travel in spirit form between two worlds. Though she lives with mortals, she can run with the gods, be aware of everything everywhere, transcend the world curtailed by death—and remember enough to bring back tales of the invisible and unknowable to those without the gift. A scant number of mortals are born with such superhuman talents: the seventh child of a seventh son or daughter is thought to have the vocation; in Hungary also a 12th child, and the youngest of 12 also holds significant powers in the Slavic world, including the ability to protect us all from witchcraft. The *táltos* of Hungarian folklore are formed in their mother's womb and born with a sign that they are predestined for healing and a life interpenetrated by spirits: an extra finger, perhaps teeth or even a tail. Their status is confirmed by a vision at age 7 or 13, and they may not resist the call to be their community's point of contact with the world of spirit. In other places and times, visionaries were similarly extreme: very beautiful, very young, very melancholic or very pious.

For Matthew Arnold, in his poem "To a Gipsy Child By the Seashore" (1845), the mediator between worlds and time zones is condemned to a solitary, melancholic existence. Because of his “soul-searching vision”, the child has “fathom’d life too far”; he has “known too much—or else forgotten all”. To theologians in the 16th and 17th centuries, the seer’s visions were of Satan’s doing, for though he had chosen to forgo his goodness, the demon retained his angelic omniscience. The gifts of the Greek prophetess Cassandra (“she who entangles men”) should be a blessing, but bring her only pain and punishment. Though she has the ability to predict the fate of her lovers and the fall of the great city of Troy, she can do nothing about it and it drives her insane. Where witches can exert control over destiny, those with second sight may only be able to report back.

previous page: ***Cassandra*, Frederick Sandys, 1904, British**

Cassandra can see future horrors, but not act on them. In some stories she gained her gift as a newborn infant. She was placed in a nest of snakes, who licked her ears so clean she could hear beyond this world.

St. Joan, the warrior witch

"Thou shalt not suffer a witch to live."

EXODUS 22:18

The brave young woman we now know as St. Joan (1412–1431) was marked out as a witch because of the voices in her head, and her belief that these voices had greater authority than the church. Joan of Arc claimed that she first experienced visions and voices at the age of 12. As she wandered the fields near her home in rural Lorraine, Saints Catherine, Margaret and Michael instructed her to save demoralized France from defeat by the English and bring the uncrowned monarch Charles to his coronation. The voices told her to dress like a man to accomplish her mission. Her predictions of the outcome of battles convinced the Dauphin, and she was given leave to dress as a knight and take titular command of the army. The 17-year-old peasant girl was regarded as an envoy of God and a gifted tactician, and under her co-command French forces scored remarkable victories, culminating with the Siege of Orléans and coronation of Charles VII at Reims cathedral.

Joan was captured by the English in 1430 and handed over to the church to be tried as a witch for her superhuman strength and foresight. At first they could find no evidence against her, but the English strove to have her condemned to prove that the French king's crown was the work of the devil and knock the confidence of the French troops. It didn't stand in her favour that she admitted at her trial to dancing at a fairy tree as a girl, that her grandmother was reputed to have seen fairies and that her role as saviour of a ruined France had been foreseen a generation earlier by mystic prophetess Marie of Avignon. Her prophesying saints were denounced as familiars and she was branded a witch. On 30 May, 1431, she was condemned to death by burning. In front of the stake and the faggots of the fire stood a sign declaring her sins—liar, heretic, sorceress and devil-worshipper—alongside her name "Jehanne La Pucelle", Joan the Maid, or Virgin: this should have been enough to nullify her trial, for a virgin was considered incapable of making a pact with the devil.

The 19-year-old Jean was tied to the stake wearing a pointed witch's hat, but her cries as the flames licked were so devout that they reputedly brought the crowd to tears. Strange phenomena were reported: the word "Jesus" written in the flames; a white dove flying from the fire; and even the executioner confessed that he had "burned a saint". Afterwards, her remains were carefully picked up, reburned and disposed of in the Seine, should any tiny pieces be used as holy relics or for magic practices.

In 1920 Joan of Arc was canonized, her prophetic visions finally accepted as signs of her holiness. And so the witch was brought into the Christian fold where she remains a potent symbol of female power, the struggle against oppression and fervent patriotism.

"...she at length confessed that she bad a familiar angel of God, which, by many conjectures, and proofs, and by the opinion of the most learned men, was judged to be an evil spirit; so that this spirit rendered her a sorceress; wherefore they permitted her to be burned at the stake by the common hangman..."

JOAN'S CONFESSION FROM *FORMICATIUS*, JOHANN NIDER

right: ***Joan of Arc at the Stake*, Artist unknown, 20th century, French**
Joan of Arc being burned at the stake, her eyes raised heavenward as her executioners pile up and stake the faggots. Though the popular image of "the Burning Times" is one of execution by burning, in many countries condemned witches were hanged.

Jehanne
heretique

Mother Shipton

"The world to an end will come,
In eighteen hundred and eighty one."

"MOTHER SHIPTON" FORECAST

The prophetess Ursula Shipton, the Yorkshire Sibyl, who reputedly lived between 1488 and 1561, is said to have foretold the future with astonishing accuracy. She "saw" carriages without horses, thoughts flying around the globe in the twinkling of an eye, men walking underwater and in the air, and iron floating on the sea. An uncanny accuracy, until you learn that the first manuscripts recording her feats don't appear until 80 years after her supposed death, and "lost scrolls" turn up at regular intervals with surprising additions, including references to the 20th century's two world wars. "New" prophesies turn up on the internet, transcribed from "forgotten" manuscripts; one describes the events of 9/11. Nevertheless, at the time of publication, Mother Shipton's prophesies are said to have caused popular excitement, even panic. When cheap chap-books and almanacs reported her predictions of earthquakes, tempests and floods, crowds gathered to witness them strike towns. Crowds gather today at the place of her birth, which is equally mysterious, being a cave of fairy repute by the river Nidd in Yorkshire close to a petrifying well that turns objects to stone. Some time before giving birth here, Ursula's mother, Agatha Sontheil, had flown on dragons and met the devil exchanging sex for magic formulae, allowing him have his way with her morning and evening in exchange for magic formulae.

The half-demonic huge, "morose" baby Mother Shipton, so the pamphlets go, was attended by imps in the shape of apes, and buffoted by all manner of strangeness: objects would fly around the home and one day, before she could walk, the baby prophetess went missing. After a great hunt, she was discovered, in her cot, stuck on a shelf halfway up the inside of the chimney (a traditional place to conceal anti-witch devices). The young Mother Shipton was an infant prodigy, no sooner shown a primer than she could read, and she soon began telling fortunes and divining the future, finding lost objects and predicting storms and deaths. Her first clients were neighbours, then the great and the good, and finally the church and state. Regardless of status, they reputedly puzzled over her riddles, which seem to foretell of key events in the reigns of kings, from Henry VIII to Charles II. They included wars and peace treaties, the Reformation and the English Civil War, beheadings and the Great Fire of London.

The details of Mother Shipton's life are just as riddling—none of her dates can be verified—but if we study the face depicted on her pamphlet of 1663, it's obvious why. Crooked body, hooked nose, crescent-moon chin? She's Mother Goose, spinner of tall tales and associated with new year predictions from her appearances in pantomime. And she's also the puppet Mr Punch, who in 16th-and 17th-century Europe was considered the archtype of a fool.

following page: ***Mother Shipton in a Reindeer-drawn Carriage*, from *Wonderful Magazine*, Artist unknown, 18th century, British**

Mother Shipton borrows the best-known mode of transport of another supernatural being, Father Christmas. *Wonderful Magazine* was an early 19th-century treasure-trove of curiosities.

WONDERFU

O'Keefe delin.

MOTHER SHIPTON'S *favori*

Pub.d

Wilkes Sculp.

mode of TRAVELLING.

nson.

Gazing globes

Crystal-gazing is an age-old technique for revealing concealed worlds, including truths held deep within the psyche, our hidden underworld. The technique has been used by seekers the world over, from aboriginal Australians, Indian yogic sages and Inca and Aztec adepts to modern healers, who might use it to diagnose and treat illness and heal energy imbalances. Precious and semi-precious stones·have always been valued for their links to the spirit world and nature's innate healing powers. For divining, practitioners of scrying often use light-catching globes or "shew stones", formed from highly polished, transparent semi-precious stones.

The properties of quartz or beryl particularly suit them to scrying. The pink form of beryl, Morganite, though not named for her, alludes to the powers of the Arthurian sorceress and healer Morgan le Fay, who has the power of flight and transformation. It is appreciated for its clarity of vision (its surface is more reflective than quarz) and is used by crystal healers to encourage boundaries to melt away and to make the impossible seem possible; it also offers insight into troubling issues. Amethyst, a purple form of quartz, encourages clear thinking and offers protection. Aventurine, quartz's sparkling green form, is thought to enhance perception, while bloodstone encourages clairvoyant skills and blue quartz brings down barriers to communication.

right: **Detail from *The Crystal Ball*, John William Waterhouse, early 20th century, British**

The young woman uses the light refracting qualities of the crystal ball to enter other worlds of perception and understanding.

Mirror magic

The Egyptian goddess Hathor is purported to have created the first mirror used for scrying or looking into the future. Her highly polished shield reflected life not as mortals see it, but as it actually is. It is this clear-sightedness that we desire when scrying. It might be thought of as a way of stepping through the looking glass into a more perfect world where anything is possible—the world that the Lady of Shalot views through her mirror but must die when she enters. A mirror is magical by nature because it creates a second "you", and in this altered state you might reveal traits that you cannot own up to in the temporal world. The Japanese fox-witch *kitsune* can only be seen making her transformation through a mirror. Some say the mirror reveals your soul, which is why it is such bad luck to break one.

Home divination with mirrors often conjures the image of a future lover: from Scotland to Russia, a girl might be advised to sit in front of a mirror by candlelight with her hair loosened, as if to undo the ties that bind her to the everyday world; she might have to eat an apple (a love token) or brush her hair (a form of hypnotism). After a quiet time of waiting, she will be enlightened by a glimpse of her intended in the mirror, as if he were standing behind her. The mirror might be angled to give a view of the Full Moon, since mirror divination is steeped in night-time rites and the bedroom arts.

In fairy tales, a mirror can reveal not the truth we would wish to see, but unwelcome home truths. Snow White's witch-like stepmother casts for compliments when she consults her oracle, the mirror on the wall. But like Hathor's mirror, it speaks the truth: she is not the fairest in the land. In the Scottish Snow-White story

"Gold-Tree and Silver-Tree", the clairvoyant truth-teller is a talking trout in a well; in the Armenian tale "Nourie Hadig" it is the New Moon in the sky, that the witch consults monthly, just as the menstrual period causes us to look within each month. In a North African tale "Rimonah of the Flashing Sword" it is, perhaps most tellingly of all, the queen's own mouth that speaks the words of truth as she looks into a porcelain bowl filled with water.

The mirror device serves to heighten the witch-queen's duplicity; there are also two of her when she adopts the clothes of a crone and peddler-woman (both witch guises) in order to lure Snow White to her death. And all the queen's lures are carefully selected to appeal to the teenage Snow White's growing narcissism: laces for a corset; an apple, the fruit of original sin; and companion of the looking glass, a comb. Mirrors in stories have signified the ills of narcissism since Ovid told us of Narcissus, who caught sight of his reflection in a pool and fell so hopelessly in love with himself that he stopped still and died. If the queen's narcissism kick-starts the Snow White story, then the daughter's narcissism almost ends the tale, causing a paralysis that apes death. The mirror is a portal to the underworld in many cultures; places where one could see one's reflection in the Earth, such as still ponds or frozen lakes, might suggest another you under the waves or beneath the Earth, and a reflection seen in reverse suggests the opposite of life: death and the spirit zone. Moving water cuts the reflection, which may be why Dorothy's pail of water in *The Wizard of Oz* is so effective in melting the Wicked Witch of the West.

following page: ***Fantasy Kiss*, Peter Newell, 1905, British**

The diviner calls up her beloved using the medium of steam.

Scrying

Scrying is the art of looking into another dimension—past, future or a present elsewhere—and learning something that can inform life in the here and now. It might provide answers to questions about love and marriage, health and prosperity, journeys or threats to person or property. This is an art as much as a gift given at birth, and can be cultivated and imitated. Mere mortals can engage in scrying as well as prophetesses. Being a skill of clear-vision, scrying requires a translucent, reflective surface—traditional media include a clear pool of water or oil (a method known as water-casting), a silver- or black-faced looking glass; a piece of burnished metal or dark stone, or the blade of a sword. It may help to illuminate the surface from behind with soft candlelight. Messages may also be received via other elements, such as a candle flame, a frozen lake, smoke and steam, burning coals, or bubbles in a simmering pot. To receive the vision, the seeker clears her mind of all but her intent, then focuses on or just beyond the clear surface. The aim is to find the soft, unfocused gaze of meditation rather than the intense concentration of study. Those who have developed a skill might intuit changes in colour or irregularities in form, faint ripples or a cloudy glow, even a mist, that suggests an image of what has passed or is to come. Others might make contact with a spirit as they tune out of the outside world and into a calm, clear inner space; this spirit may reveal truths or answer questions, perhaps in a "vision" that appears before the reflective surface. The difficulty of attuning ordinary eyes to this more subtle form of perception is revealed in its name—the term "scrying" means "to make out dimly".

“She possessed a wonderful mirror, which could answer her when she stood before it and said—
‘Mirror mirror, upon the wall,
Who is the fairest of all?’
The mirror answered:
‘Thou, O queen, art the fairest of all.’
and the queen was contented because she knew the mirror could speak nothing but the truth.”

“LITTLE SNOW WHITE”, IN *GRIMM’S FAIRY TALES*, L. L. WEEDON (TRANS.)

left: ***The Queen and the Magic Mirror*, William Henry Margetson, 1916, British**

A snake-like symbol hides the mirror from prying eyes, while signposting the queen’s primal wickedness.

Divination days

Certain days of the year are considered more auspicious than others for divination. They tend to coincide with festivals devoted to the spirit realm and the dead souls gathered at its door awaiting admittance. Hallowe'en is the most obvious. This is also the cusp between the old and new years in the Celtic (and Wiccan) calendar. Potential is heightened at new years, so what better time to divine future fortune? A cake might be baked containing charms that allocate luck for the coming year: a ring for love, a coin for prosperity and a rag for its opposite. Nuts might be placed in the fire or a bowl of water to answer questions by flaming, popping or sinking.

The 12 days from Christmas to Epiphany are, from Europe to Central Asia, another time when the dead and spirits are coursing through the skies and a new year turns. This period was once dedicated to Hera as goddess of death, and since at least the 4th century has been celebrated in a similarly unruly way to Hallowe'en, with guising, begging at doors, conjuring and divination games. The apparitions abroad may bring predictions—Charles Dickens' fortune-telling Christmas ghost story *A Christmas Carol* (1843) is the best known of a long tradition. To find out what the spirits predict, on the stroke of midnight, witches and mortals may tip molten lead or wax into a container of cold water. Once new year wishes have been exchanged and the substance has cooled, its shape can be observed for clues, perhaps by placing a light behind to cast a shadow on a wall, as in Russia and Finland. Regular folks might see the shape of a house or a boat, a heart or church, a bag of money or a footprint; the gifted might find significance in seemingly inconsequential bubbles of wax.

Merchant's Gargling Oil Almanac

Dream and Fate Book

The wryd sisters

Classical mythology tells of a group of three goddesses who hold our destiny in their hands. The first, depicted with a spindle, spins out the thread of our lives; the second has a measure to tell the length of our days; and the third a pair of scissors to snip us off at our allotted time. They are sometimes said to govern time past (neatly balled on the spindle), time present (being teased through the fingers), and time to come (the untidy raw yarn fluffed on the distaff). In northern European mythology, the threads of fate are spun out by three virgin giantesses "huge of might" known as the Norns, who form the wryd, the warp and weft of life (the term *wyrd* may derive from words meaning to "turn", "grow" or "become"). Popularly, one Norn deals in what has become, the second what is becoming and the third what must be. These witches visit each newborn in the night to set the warp threads onto the loom of destiny. But the weave, the weft thread, is not predetermined; its pattern is influenced by our deeds, both past and future. In a manner similar to the law of karma, our past choices make us what we are and shape the future, but we have the freedom to begin a new pattern in each successive present moment.

In Roman mythology, the three fates, or "wyrd sisters", are the Parcae, for whom citizens left out a meal with three knives on certain nights of the year. Failing to placate the witches of fate can be risky, as the parents of Sleeping Beauty find out when they fail to invite the 13th fairy to the celebration of their daughter's birth. Uglyane (no wonder they didn't invite her; she's obviously a witch) turns up regardless. She curses the child to prick her finger on a spindle (the weapon of the fates) and fall down dead. The 12th fairy commutes her term to a deep sleep of one hundred years. In the early modern era, when witchcraft trials peaked, similar social faux-pas are mentioned many times in witness reports. In one case, parents stated that their baby was bewitched by a woman not invited to a christening; in another case, sheep suffered after the suspected witch was excluded from a sheering dinner. Unlike Sleeping Beauty's parents, the people at these trials understood that an old woman scorned has the power to meddle with fate.

"Thence come the maidens mighty in wisdom,
Three from the dwelling down 'neath the tree;

Urth is one named, Verthandi the next,
On the wood they scored, and Skuld the third.
Laws they made there, and life allotted
To the sons of men, and set their fates."

"VOLUSPO, THE WISE-WOMAN'S PROPHECY" IN *THE POETIC EDDA* (WRITTEN DOWN 1000–1300) TRANS. HENRY ADAMS BELLOWS

previous page: **Detail from *Gargling Oil Almanac*, Artist unknown, 1886, British**

A print advertisement for an almanac for 1886 shows a woman sitting with a wise old owl on a crescent Moon. What else could she be but a beguiling and sage witch?

**"Mightily wove they the web of fate,
While Bralund's towns were trembling all;
And there the golden threads they wove,
And in the moon's hall fast they made him."**

***THE FIRST LAY OF HELGI HUNDINGSBANE*, TRANS. HENRY ADAMS BELLOWS (AFTER 10TH CENTURY)**

right: ***The Fates Gathering in the Stars*, Elihu Vedder, late 19th century, American**

Three fates pull in the warp and weft of the Universe. Their spindles lie ready at their feet.

Thousand-year-old voices

"Beginning with the generation first
Of mortal men down to the very last
I'll prophesy each thing what erst has been,
And what is now, and what shall yet befall
The world through the impiety of men."

THE SIBYLLINE ORACLES **(*c.*150 BCE–*c.*300 CE)**

The Sibyls were prophetesses of a far-distant past, possibly from as early as the 6th-century BCE, whose words of truth still echo through the tales woven around them and the places they inhabited. There were reputedly ten or even twelve prophetesses scattered around the known world—at Delphi and Rome, in Persia and Libya—and ranging in age, though many had gained the wisdom that comes with great age. They lived in caves from where they sang their prophesies, says Virgil, recording their verses and casting rune-like symbols on oracles, palm leaves that were carried on the breeze out through the entrances of the grottoes. Some say the Sibyls conjured up the alphabet and invented Greek alphabet divination, others that they conducted tours of the underworld. But what their *Sibylline Verses* actually foretold we can only second-guess, since none survive. Some of the leaves were collected in books the Cumaean Sibyl is said to have burned; the remaining books were acquired by Rome and kept in a temple, where they were consulted by opening at random when the empire was in need of healing. But a temple fire destroyed them. The collection was remade, stitched together from material gleaned from all corners of the empire and housed in a new temple, dedicated to Apollo, principal god of prophesy. These tomes, too, were lost, after the temple closed in the 5th century. But fragments have emerged in languages including Arabic and Ethiopic retelling some of the Sibyls' prophesies, including of Christ's virgin birth and the fall of Troy. Intricately embroidered legends of the Sibyls' lives have emerged, too.

The two most story-woven Sibyls are the beautiful Delphic Sibyl and the Cumaean Sibyl. The latter, who inhabited a Greek colony near Naples in Italy, is so fêted that she may be referred to simply as "the Sibyl". Ovid tells how she came about her powers, when the smitten Apollo offered to grant her heart's desire. Grabbing handfuls of dust, she asked for as many years' life as the grains between her palms. But she neglected to ask for eternal youth; she loses her form first to age and then to the elements until there is only her voice left, bringing the truth to light from deep within a cave. The Cumaean Sibyl's biography has been much coloured; folk and fairy-tale motifs cling to it, as do tales of pilgrimage and questing. In some tales, devotees of magic-making journey to her grotto to pay homage. They describe how, after creeping through a long passage into her inner sanctum, they reach a paradise filled with feasting and sensuous pleasure. But it seems to be governed by fairy laws, for it can turn monstrous in a blink, as those worlds are apt to do. Modern-day pilgrims can venture there still, entering the Sibyl's labyrinthine underworld near a Greek acropolis at Cumae and wondering at the "hundred gateways and hundred wide mouths" which Virgil described as the portals for ageless wisdom.

"The sun had now set. The owl flew into the thicket, and directly afterwards there came out of it a crooked old woman, yellow and lean, with large red eyes and a hooked nose, the point of which reached to her chin."

"JORINDE AND JORINGEL", *THE GREEN FAIRY BOOK*, THE GRIMM BROTHERS
ED. ANDREW LANG

previous page: ***The Cumaean Sybil*, Elihu Vedder, late 19th century, American**
The Cumaean Sibyl in this picture stalks the landscape with her prophesies gathered to her breast. Like many of Elihu Vedder's landscapes, this painting has a visionary quality.

right: **Fairy Tale illustration, Walter Crane, 19th century, British**
Witches have distinctive eyes with which to look into the future and raise fear in their prey. This witch by Walter Crane is flanked by two fearsome turkeys, and their eyes resemble one another. The Italian word for a witch, *strega*, perhaps drawn from the Latin *strix*, "little owl", makes a similar connection.

The power of fascination

"Big is their head, goggle their eyes, their beaks are formed for rapine, their feathers blotched with grey, their claws fitted with hooks."

ON THE *STRIGES* FROM *FASTI*, *BOOK* 6, OVID

There is something about the eyes that marks out a witch; something that suggests she can see beyond the everyday and into forever. The irises may be startlingly blue, the pupil double, the whites tinged red; she may shoot fiery or penetrating glances and be unable to shed cleansing tears. The dread power of such mesmerizing eyes is referred to as "fascination"—the word may derive from Greek via the Latin *fascinato*, meaning the mysterious power of the eyes—and is considered peculiar to the female form of glamour. It was once believed that a witch gained control over souls, especially the victims of love spells, by holding the gaze, impressing her thoughts and desires directly onto the heart. The Greek philosopher Democritus believed that the eyes provided a way in and out of the body for a thin fluid that brought about misfortune.

Visual enthralment is analogous with the evil eye. Those considered in greatest need of protection from being "overlooked" are the most beautiful, the most fortunate and the most happy: newborn infants, delightful children and radiant brides. Praising any of them too highly rouses the attention of the eye; even thinking thoughts of praise may open a conduit that it can use. Farm animals are susceptible, especially horses, cows and pigs, and so too are those who work on the sea. Amuletic ornaments were prescribed in ancient Egypt and are common still today in the near East to protect the vulnerable from "eye-biting". Whether worn, painted onto boats or suspended at windows, on animals and in cars, they tend to be made of reflective talismanic metals formed into crescent-Moon shapes, resembling the curve of an almond-shaped eye. Or simple blue glass beads (perhaps inset with yellow and white "pupils") may be used, so shiny that they dazzle the eye with its own evil. Even a blue cord will suffice (the "something blue" of the bride).

Eyes and evil are also linked in the image of the owl, bird of wisdom, bird of prey and omen of misfortune: to Roman soothsayers, the owl's call signified a death to come. Ovid tells of *striges*, hideous, misshapen old women transformed into birds of prey, who roam the night skies, their eyes swivelling to detect unweaned infants to snatch from the cradle. Screech owls, in particular, have been thought interchangeable with witches, for their eerie shrieks, silent flight, night navigation and, importantly, for their all-seeing eyes. In the classical world, they were sacred to the Greek goddess of wisdom, Athene, described by Homer as "owl-eyed". In some native American cultures, the owl is a bird of visioning that guides those in trances towards the higher knowledge of the spirit world.

Early dread-eyed soothsayers of Greek mythology include the triple-formed Graeae, a trio of hideous old women (they were born aged), who lived deep in a forest within a dark cave, only coming out at night. Though they had only one eye—which they passed between them—it was all-seeing, able to augur the future of mortals. Many ventured into the forest to look upon their horrible form and gain

insight, including the hero Perseus, who stole the eye to force the sisters to give up their secret knowledge. He used their wisdom to seek out and slay the Gorgon, three more monstrous sisters with eyes so piercing they might turn a man to stone. After Perseus severs the head of one of them, the Medusa, the power of its stare remains so intense that it was mounted on Athene/Minerva's breastplate as a protective shield, and replicas were created in public places to zap the evil eye. The single-eye, like that of the Graeae, is to this day considered the mark of the witch in some cultures. Others liken it to the single "eye" of the cervix, which guards the dark entrance to the womb, the site both of uniquely female power and the future of mankind.

left: ***Perseus and Graiae*, Helen Stratton, early 20th century, British**
The trio of women who were born aged refused to tell Perseus how to find the Gorgon until the hero steals their one shared eye and threatens to leave them blinded.

following page: **Detail from *Woman Performing a Bloodletting*, Artist unknown, 17th century, Dutch**
A 17th-century depiction of a wise woman carrying out a blood-letting, part of accepted medical practice at the time.

Cunning folk

The word "cunning" derives from the Anglo-Saxon *cunnan*, "to know". Cunning women and men were those in the know—about how to heal and how to attract love, about what the future held, the whereabouts of lost objects and the identity of thieves. Their knowledge was either passed through the family, like a trade or could be studied—for those who could read, in works of astrology and almanacs, herbals and fortune-telling chapbooks; for others, through an informal apprenticeship. Ownership of this knowledge could bring in a useful living, and research suggests that in late 16th-century Essex no one lived more than 16 km (10 miles) from a cunning person. Other skills came with experience—how to tweak stock herbal remedies to suit individuals, diagnosing sickness in animals, the signs of early pregnancy and the stages of childbirth. One prime piece of expertise (it commanded the best price) was the ability to diagnose the symptoms of witchcraft, identify its source and prescribe an antidote to the effects of enchantment. A wise woman might do a urine analysis or water divination to determine the cause, then decide to draw a curse out of the body and transfer it elsewhere, perhaps into an animal. She might guide the patient back to health with herbal remedies to relieve physical ailments, amulets to soothe the mind and Bible tracts to ease the spirit. She might also choose to name and shame a suspect witch, or destroy her by performing acts of countermagic on her belongings. But the wise woman was not a witch herself. Though cunning folk used many of the stock skills of a witch—herbs, sympathetic magic, word spells, protective charms, scrying—they could not bewitch. I can "not witche" testified the cunning woman of St Osyth, Ursula Kemp in 1582; I can only "unwitche". She was hung nevertheless.

The first detectives

Cunning folk might be thought of as the first detectives, says the historian Owen Davies. With their scrying skills, position of authority and knowledge of a community's inner workings, they were able to unlock all manner of mysteries. They were paid to locate missing goods and people and solve crimes from burglary to extortion. And the business paid well, prices set on a sliding tariff according to the value of the missing object, reputation of the client and number of toes that might be stepped on. It would cost more again to have items magically returned. These activities caused considerable consternation to the authorities; so good was the word of cunning folk in a community that summary justice might be meted out—with all the social discord that might follow. Though once word got round that a wise woman was involved, objects often mysteriously turned up.

Detective methods included scrying using a mirror, ball or smoke—the world of these early Sherlock Holmes was as hazy as the misty streets where Conan Doyle's hero conjured up his clues. The sieve and shears method was also popular. A sieve balanced on a pair of shears or set spinning would turn or fall on hearing the suspect's name. The same technique could be used with a Bible or psalter hung from a key. Treasure-seeking was a popular service offered by cunning folk in early modern Europe. In rural areas, people with valuables often buried them to keep them safe from prying eyes (they still do), and cunning folk might be charged to find them, perhaps using dowsing rods or by contacting spirits to ask for advice and directions. This again commanded a good price before popular chapbooks, in France especially, published step-by-step instructions that made it a DIY sport.

Cunning folk gained a reputation for the power of their performance. With so many to choose from in cities especially, it became a profession that required a calling card. A wise woman's USP might be elaborate ceremonies involving outsized volumes of spells (the older-looking the better) or artfully arranged parchments marked with magic symbols or foreign words in red and black ink. Her book of spells was an impressive part of her trade—especially to those who could not read—and so she protected it jealously, displayed it ostentatiously and used it flamboyantly. Other wise women were known for their stagey declamation of incantations or the gravitas and reassurance added to their work by adaptation of solemn religious ritual. One Yorkshire wise woman was renowned for her outlandish garb, including swirling robes and a conical hat that must have disturbed the magical herbs drying from the rafters. The sceptical commentator Reginald Scot wrote off these practitioners of "crafty science" as counterfeiters and tricksters who practised sleight of hand to manipulate and swindle the gullible. From the late 18th-century, there was a growth in the number of professional sleight-of-hand performers, street conjurors and stage magicians who combined music and illusion in the music-hall tradition. Where witches were prosecuted under witchcraft legislation, cunning folk, like these entertainers, were more likely to be prosecuted as fraudsters or vagrants. Such tricksters and "old trots" were not working for the devil (the ultimate trickster in the Christian faith) but for Mammon, passing over souls for the contents of their purses.

"Let me see how many trades I have to live by: first, I am a wise woman, and a fortune-teller, and under that I deal in physic and fore-speaking, in palmistry, and recovering of things lost; next, I undertake to cure mad folks; then I keep gentlewomen lodgers, to furnish such chambers as I let out by the night; then I am provided for bringing young wenches to bed; and, for a need, you see I play the matchmaker."

***THE WISE WOMAN OF HOGSDON*, THOMAS HEYWOOD**

left: **Detail from *Predicting the Future for Tea Sediment*, Artist Unknown, 19th century, British**

A wise woman predicts the future from the sediments of a tea cup. The client has desperation in her eyes. In *A Compleat System of Magick* (1726), Daniel Defoe noted, "'tis not their cunning but their clients want of cunning, that gives them the least appearance of common sense in all their practice".

Gipsy fortune

Romany folk began to arrive in Western Europe from the Balkans and Spain in the late 15th century, where they were greeted with suspicion for their looks, language and itinerant lifestyle, and persecuted by Egyptians Acts that forced them to the periphery of communities, socially and geographically. They went to the same places witches were thought to lurk: outside the perimeter fence or boundary road and on the edge of the woods; later, many were transported to the "new" world. By popular conception, Romany folk were descended from the inventors of the apparatus of formal magic—the ancient Egyptians—though their heritage can, in fact, be traced to the Indus Valley in the 9th century. Romany families prize their psychic ability—all are thought to inherit the gift of second sight—and their cunning in making a living by wedding it to the performance skills is also said to be in the Romany blood. *Dukkering*, the art of fortune-telling performance, is still taught to girls today from a young age rather than formal schooling, to equip them to join the family business. They serve an apprenticeship in four divining skills: palmistry, reading tea leaves, scrying with a crystal ball and telling the cards, alongside astrology, story-telling and other skills of the show-woman. The most skilled in these matters are called *chovihani/o*, or witch (a Russian spell-caster is a *charovnik*). The role is a sacred one, involving responsibility for the spiritual well-being of a community, and one is born to it. Cunning women in the past claimed to have acquired their skills from gypsy witches, a respected way to become a wise woman, since Romany folk were renowned for undoing witch's spells much later than settled peoples. "Green doctors", gipsy healers, were also famed for their cures.

Romany fortune-tellers are best known for hawking their craft in places where people gather outdoors: markets, festivals, fairgrounds, race meetings and seaside piers. Originally, they attracted trade by wearing red; this extended to encompass semi-permanent tents or booths as richly adorned as their garments and gold jewellery. The stalls recall 19th-century descriptions of wise women in Eastern Europe, who adorned stalls on the feast days of Saints John and George, Christmas and Easter with boughs of greenery and flower wreaths, a sign that they were open for trade in magic.

As Western Europe became increasingly urbanized, the Romany lifestyle—living close to and lightly on the land and in harmony with the seasons—became appealing for romantically minded aesthetes; in the early 19th century, there was a craze for learning a little Romany, and for befriending and describing Romany folk in paint or words. The nature poet John Clare was entranced by their life, which seemed to him indivisible from nature. In his poem "The Gipsies", he describes an old lady "tawny with the smoke" who is so at one with her landscape —her fire, the wind, the trees—that, like the wood witches of Scandinavian lore, she has mastery over it. She can split open the old oak tree, repository of magical powers, and has dominion over game: rabbits give themselves up willingly to her. If you are at one with the natural world, the signs that the Universe sends, whether circling birds or leaves in a tea cup, must be attended to.

following page: ***La bonne aventure [Good Fortune]*, L. Boilly, 1824, French**

Caricature of a fortune-teller.

La bonne aventure

“[the gipsy’s] strange talk, voice, manner, had by this time wrapped me in a kind of dream. One unexpected sentence came from her lips after another, till I got involved in a web of mystification…”

***JANE EYRE*, CHARLOTTE BRONTË**

“The gypsy fortune-teller is accustomed for years to look keenly and earnestly into the eyes of those whom she *dukkers* or ‘fortune-tells’. She is accustomed to make ignorant and credulous or imaginative girls feel that her mysterious insight penetrates ‘with a power and with a sign’ to their very souls. As she looks into their palms, and still more keenly into their eyes, while conversing volubly with perfect self-possession, ere long she observes that she has made a hit—has chanced upon some true passage or relation to the girl’s life. This emboldens her. Unconsciously the Dream Spirit, or the Alter-Ego, is awakened. It calls forth from the hidden stores of Memory strange facts and associations, and with it arises the latent and often unconscious quickness of Perception, and the gypsy actually apprehends and utters things which are ‘wonderful’. There is no clairvoyance, illumination or witchcraft in such cases.”

***GYPSY SORCERY AND FORTUNE-TELLING*, CHARLES GODFREY LELAND**

A family profession

Interview with Claire Petulengro

A member of one of the most famous of clairvoyant Romany families, Claire is a clairvoyant and astrologer who has been reading palms since the age of six. She writes horoscopes for publications including *The Mirror, Company* and more than 40 UK regional newspapers, and is on-line astrologer for VH-1 and the phone technology company 3. She was resident astrologer at the Express Newspaper Group for over three years and for *OK!* magazine for over five years. Claire has broadcast on Sky, ITV, BBC and Channel 4, including *The Big Breakfast*, *This Morning* and *Richard and Judy*, and is the author of a number of best-selling books on astrology.

You come from a line of renowned clairvoyants.

I come from a very close-knit Romany family. My mother was born in a *vardo* (wagon), and didn't move into bricks and mortar until her early 20s. In the old days, the extended family moved from town to town. It wasn't until World War II that this lifestyle became impossible. Though life for Romanies in Britain was nowhere near as difficult as in Europe (the Nazi regime executed tens of thousands of Romanies), there was suspicion here, and it was no longer safe to turn up in a town as strangers. The family split up, the sisters displaced to various seaside towns—Blackpool, Skegness, Brighton—where there was a constant influx of visitors. My mother became very well known in Brighton: she gave readings to the royal family, stars of stage and screen, and would jet out to the States to do readings for celebrities such as Michael Caine and Joan Collins.

How did you start doing readings?

My mother saw some clients at home, and when I was still small—about six years of age—she took me into the room and asked "What do you feel about this lady?" I would pick up on a client's feelings; that she felt very sad or had lost something. Romanies teach that we should trust a child's intuition, and nurture it; we should keep ourselves open to a world full of possibilities. It's not witchcraft, but about trusting your feelings.

Did this set you out as different from other children?

I always knew I was different, but didn't know exactly how until I got to school. I was like a little wise woman, skinny and tall with old-fashioned glasses, who knew about things the other kids didn't. For instance, if I had a headache, I wouldn't take a pill, but treat it with herbs, such as feverfew and natural remedies, like fresh air. My grandmother was a herbalist. Obviously it's difficult when you stand out as a child; but if I thought about it, I felt proud and special.

Are you bringing up your own children in the Romany ways?

When my little boy Paris was three years old, we were returning home from an afternoon out. He was in the back seat of the car and I sat up front texting a friend to see if we had left his coat at her house (we hadn't talked about it). He leaned forward, touched my hair and said, "Silly Mummy! I know where my coat is—in my bedroom." "How did you know what I was doing?" I asked (he couldn't read). "I can hear you in my head", he said. He's got the gift. I'm teaching him to use it to listen to his instinct—to find out what will make him happy. Then he'll have the most wonderful of lives. I'm bringing my children up to know their heritage—but it's up to them what they do with this knowledge.

I didn't realize what a special gift I had until I was 13, when a friend of my mother's told me: "You need only ask for something and say you're willing to pay the price and it will come to you". I was in a youth drama group rehearsing *The Lion, the Witch and the Wardrobe*, understudying the part of Susan, but what I wanted more than anything was to play Susan. So I asked for it, swearing on my life. At the very next class, we were told that the understudies would share the performances with the main actors. I swore then that I would never use this power again. But when my little girl was gravely ill in hospital, I asked God to make her better and said I would give whatever it took. She recovered next day, and when I got home, on the doormat was a letter from my agent asking if I wanted to take part in a trek along the Great Wall of China to support childrens' charities. I was unable to leave on the day everyone else was going, but they agreed I could arrive later, since I was so sure I was supposed to take part. Who should meet me on my eventual arrival but the expedition leader. Our eyes locked and now we're happily married.

Romanies are great believers in karma and in God. Even when Romanies were illiterate and didn't go to school, we were taught to read using the Bible and were married in church. Whether we use herbs or astrology, we believe we should help not harm people.

You began working professionally at the age of 15.

My grandmother, Eva Petulengro Sr., had a booth on the end of Brighton's Palace Pier. When I was 15, she had a stroke. Well, the people didn't stop coming to the end of the pier, and school wasn't so important to me (my mother and uncles hadn't been to school), so I took her place. I worked from 10 am to 10 pm seven days a week, and once it was finished, I dropped the money at my grandmother's before helping out at my mother's restaurant.

Well after I took over in the booths, there were queues day and night for my readings. People couldn't believe that someone so young knew about their future and could make predictions without having much life experience. But a good astrologer or clairvoyant understands what a person needs. However, we don't hold the answers to problems. We don't have the power to change the world.

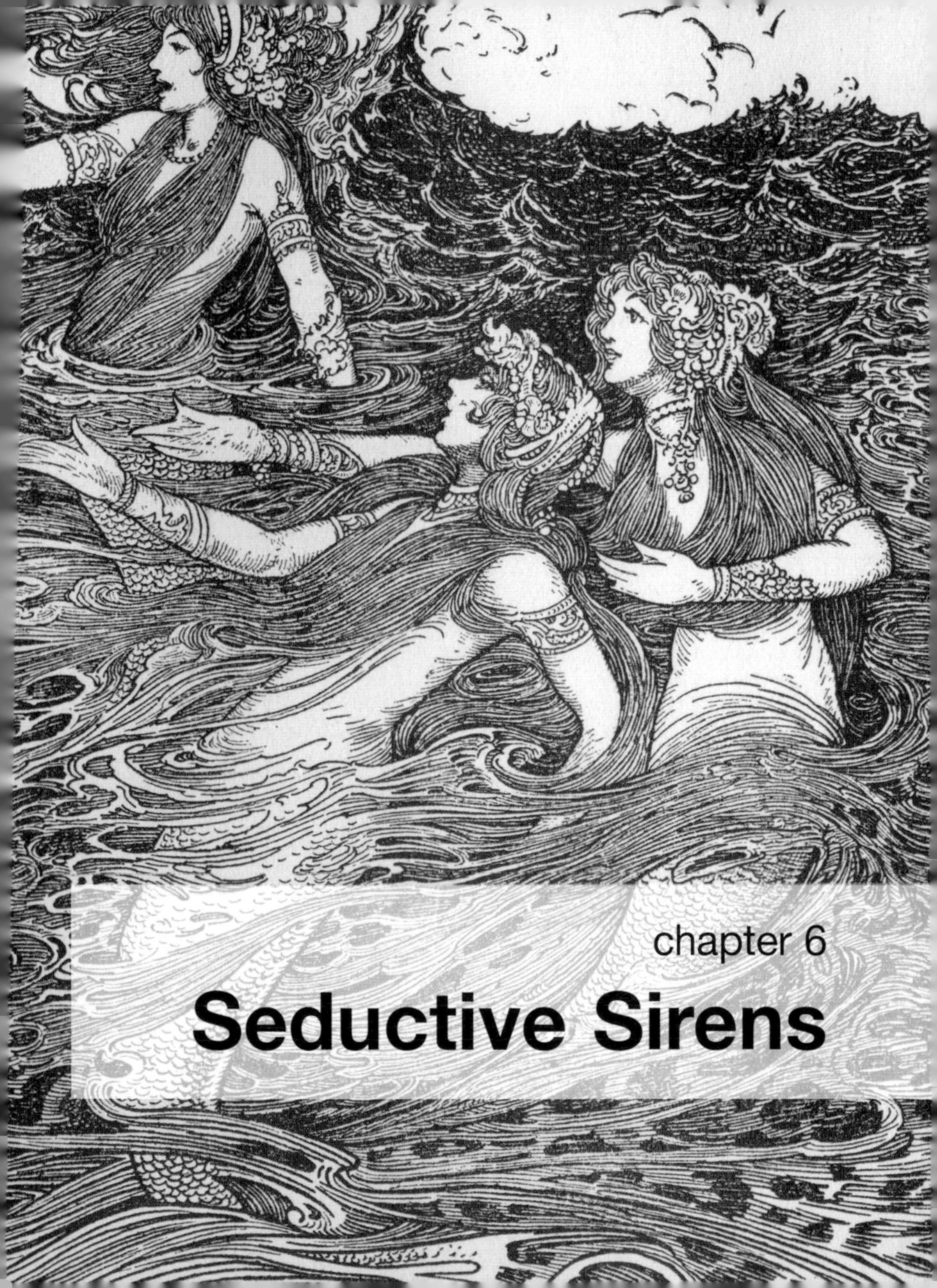

chapter 6

Seductive Sirens

Enticement and enchantment

**"Her neather partes misshapen, monstrous,
Were hidd in water, that I could not see—
But they did seeme more foule and hideous
Then womans shape would believe to bee..."**

**DESCRIPTION OF THE WITCH-LIKE DUESSA, FROM *THE FAERIE QUEENE*,
EDMOND SPENSER**

Through history, the iconography of the witch has swung between hideous crone and beguiling seductress. The siren and the mermaid belong to the latter breed. Too beautiful to be of the mortal world, a mermaid uses all the senses to entice: irresistible music, beguiling eyes, undulating curves and wet, tousled hair. Her sensuality turns a man senseless, drawing him deeper towards a silent marine underworld where mortals cannot thrive. The Greek siren drove adventurers to distraction: Odysseus's crew only escaped with their lives because the enchantress Circe warned him to stop their ears with wax. He had them tie him to the mast of the ship with strictest warnings to ignore his commands to be unbound.

previous page: ***They Swam before the Ships and Sang Lovely Songs*, Louis John Rhead, 1914, British**

Mermaids raise a storm with their mind-numbing keening and with it draw a ship towards its fate in this illustration.

"…if a man even walks in a place where witches have been he will become bewildered or mad, and remain so till driven homeward by hunger. But such places may generally be recognized by their footprints in the sand; for witches have only four toes—the great toe being wanting. These mysterious four toe-tracks, which are indeed often seen, are supposed by unbelievers to be made by wild geese, swans, or wild ducks, but in reply to this the peasant or gypsy declares that witches often take the form of such fowl."

***GYPSY SORCERY AND FORTUNE-TELLING*, CHARLES GODFREY LELAND**

The siren's seduction is always disquieting, for something about her is wrong, even if the viewer is lulled initially by her beauty. While from the Middle Ages, her beguiling upper body may be all ringlets and pert breasts, look lower, or try to explore the pleasures of the flesh that seem to be on offer, and you will discover a treacherous bite. For sirens are part animal.

As if trying to warn us that witches are closer to animal instinct and passion than mortals, they are half-fish (symbol of wanton fecundity before the oceans were over-fished) or half-bird, maybe with a serpent's tail for good measure (witches' bodies are ever-mutable). Sometimes the body of a bird-woman is an eagle's, terrifying bird of prey from whom no living creature is safe and considered an omen of death. In his *Metamorphoses*, Ovid describes how women transform themselves into birds by rubbing their limbs with magic ointment; succubi go the other way, morphing from demon to beguiling maiden to corrupt good men with naughty thoughts. They should have spotted the clue to the untamed sexuality lurking beneath the succubus' skirt: a claw or one foot made of something other than flesh. In medieval and Renaissance Europe, a goose-like webbed foot or eagle's claw spied beneath a gown was a veiled reference to the vulva, a woman's hidden parts. The Queen of Sheba, that fabulous Bibical temptress, was often painted with one webbed foot.

In 1522 Martin Luther declared that all witches should be considered whores, and in the 16th and 17th centuries, the words "mermaid" and "siren" became euphemisms for prostitutes. But however raunchy the mermaid seems, she is, perversely, a symbol of virginity. Part of her horrific power over men is that she is impenetrable; sexy but sexless. In this, she shares characteristics with the Christian mother goddess "Mary", who conceives and gives birth but remains unviolated (she might as well have a tail). The mermaid seems to unite the roles of the two Marys of the New Testament, virgin and prostitute. By uniting seeming opposites, she wrecks not just ships, but the church's neat dualism.

The shape-shifting nixe or Rhine Maiden, is a water siren from the German tradition (her Scandinavian cousins are the *näcke*, *nykk* and *nøkke*), who emerges from the river or lake each evening to lure men with ethereal instrumental music and the mesmerizing repetitive combing of her long tresses. These creatures, too, have the habit of changing form, one moment a white horse, next a fish or snake, and then maid; the change can be so quick that it leaves tell-tale signs: a dripping hem or a body strangely asymmetrical. Follow the maiden and

**"For so delicious were the words she sung,
It seem'd he had lov'd them a whole summer long:
And soon his eyes had drunk her beauty up,
Leaving no drop in the bewildering cup,
And still the cup was full—while he afraid
Lest she should vanish ere his lip had paid
Due adoration, thus began to adore."**

***LAMIA*, JOHN KEATS**

she will lead you, some say caringly, to the depths of the river or bottom of the well to assist her with her weaving. Thanks to the popularity of a ballad written by Heinrich Heine in 1823, the most famed of these freshwater maiden is the sorceress Lorelei, who haunts a rock on a treacherous bend on the banks of the Rhine.

Slavic water witches, the *rusalka*, confound their human prey with Mother Goose-like riddles before tickling them to death with playful eroticism. They emerge from their watery lair bedecked with weed and drape themselves over the branches of birch and willow trees, a vision of luminous flesh, ample breasts and wet locks that lures men and women alike. An Ukranian antidote is to carry a sprig of wormwood, the unwitching herb. Compared with the mermaid, the *rusalka* is more melancholic than malevolent, the shadow of a mortal woman who has sinned by getting pregnant out of wedlock or committing suicide, and getting her own back through the only powers left to her, seduction, for her body is fully female.

"Fishermen sometimes see her in the bright summer's sun, when a thin mist hangs over the sea, sitting on the surface of the water, and combing her long golden hair with a golden comb, or driving up her snow-white cattle to feed on the strands and small islands. At other times she comes as a beautiful maiden, chilled and shivering with the cold of the night, to the fires the fishers have kindled, hoping by this means to entice them to her love. Her appearance prognosticates both storm and ill success in their fishing."

***THE FAIRY MYTHOLOGY*, THOMAS KEIGHTLEY**

right: ***The Fisherman and the Siren*, Knut Ekvall, *c.* 1900, Swedish**
The water witch expresses her sexuality in a way that is simultaneously attractive but repulsive to mortal men. This gives her great power over the human imagination.

Alluring locks

The water siren's magical arsenal is bound up in her unbound hair. Her dishevelled, post-coital "do" drops abundantly onto her shoulders and over her breasts. She fiddles with it, twists and plaits it like the Nouns or fates playing with the threads of a man's destiny, admires it in a hand mirror and rhythmically strokes it with her comb. This last detail is revealing, for the ancient Greek word for comb is the same word used to describe the vulva. In some early writings of the Christian church, it is women who incite the rebel Watcher angels to their sexual undoing by inciting lust with their uncovered tresses.

The act of unbinding brings forth constrained powers. A Russian maiden unloosens her belt in bed before speaking magic words to allow her innate powers of divination to conjure her future beau into a dream. Traditionally in childbirth, a mother's buttons were undone and hair loosened to unlock the extra lifeforce required to ride the waves of pain and push out a baby. Unbound hair is a sign of unchained female sexuality, which is intense stuff. In one of rural Russia's most mighty charms, the women of a village were said to venture outdoors at midnight, shedding their girdles (or even their clothes) and loosening their hair to unleash their potential. They then seal that life-force into the village by pulling a plough around its boundaries anti-clockwise (an act of reversal magic). The drawn circle contained a power so intense that it could keep out the plague. Similar customs are reported in India to bring rain in times of drought.

Legend says that a witch's hair can never be cut; it will mangle the sharpest blade or scissors. Neither will it burn. Like sheep's wool, it's thought to cause a flame to shrink away. So powerful is witch hair that in description and depiction it transforms into snakes or coils of flame. Horace paints a word picture of the witch Sagana, who "bristles with streaming hair", and speaks also of Canidia, whose "locks and dishevelled head" are "entwined with short vipers". The image reaches its zenith in the Medusa's twisting locks, which are entwined with writhing serpents. Here, a woman's hair has become terrifyingly, hideously powerful, for beneath it there poke bulging eyes, a demonic teeth-baring grin, and a lasciviously extended tongue. In Greek mythology, Medusa's head was a scare-all, used as a magic shield to ward off the enemy: all who look at her turn to stone. So powerful is the Medusa's form that her public statues were covered but for a few days of the year—the sight of her could even shrivel the fruit on the trees.

following page: **Detail from *L'Eau des Sirens*, Jules Cheret, 19th century, French**

Mermaids are used to lure women, too, as in this 19th-century French advertisement for hair dye found at all the best *coiffeurs* and *parfumeurs*.

Recoloration des Cheveux

Par

L'EAU DES SIRÈNES

PLUSIEURS FOIS MÉDAILLÉE

"She claims him with her great blue eyes
She binds him with her hair;
Oh, break the spell with holy words,
Unbind him with a prayer!"

THE WITCH OF WENHAM, JOHN GREENLEAF WHITTIER

Love magic

One of the services offered by a witch or wise woman was matchmaking—by fair means or foul. Cunning folk were called upon to make introductions and also to cast enticement spells—to procure a husband, coerce an unwilling partner or fix up an ailing relationship. She might also be able to return an errant husband or force a marriage for an abandoned mother. In an era before child-support payments and prenups, this craft put the wise woman at the moral and economic heart of a community.

For wise women, there was money in love magic; it may have provided their bread-and-butter income. Checking for compatibility and finding suitors might be achieved by scrying techniques using mirrors, rings and candles (the latter have potent symbolism in the bedroom), by the balanced sieve method, or by reading auspicious signs in palms, the stars or the cards. Amulets might be advised, such as snail shells threaded into charms (with their horns and night habits, snails are associated both with witches and sex). Love potions gained in efficacy if they used the seeker's DNA in the ingredients: menstrual blood perhaps from the water from a soaked, stained garment; sweat; or the rinse water from underwear (a sympathetic magic we still call on when throwing knickers at pop idols). These ingredients were mixed with aphrodisiacs from the wise women's pharmacopoeia and were best administered to the intended by mouth. The desperate might also try to adulterate his food with blessed or charmed salt, bake a spice cake with magical incantations, or even simply breathe devotion into his wine or water. Nakedness played a part in love lore: spell books recommended nude rites for the bedroom (combing all the hair on one's body by candlelight was one) and outdoors—a dash around a standing stone might do the trick. However, provoking a person to "abnormal love" was declared a capital offence under the 1542 Witchcraft Act, and in Russia priests were asked to check for such sinful acts during confession. Today, village and internet-based wise women decline clients who request coercive love spells; they will only work their magic if both partners are involved.

At times in history, the role of wise woman, matchmaker and procuress blurred; in Germany the pejorative title "Madam" could be used of any of them. Literature is full of tales of older women training beautiful young girls in the magical art of seduction, and using them to lure clients. In Samuel Richardson's novel *Pamela* (1740), the innocent young heroine eventually finds herself in bed with her wise-woman protectress—a madam and midwife—on one side and her gentleman client (confusingly dressed as Nan the maid) on the other; the wise woman's hands and words control the situation. But it's a control sometimes welcomed as a way of easing young women through society's moral hoops: in Daniel Defoe's *Moll Flanders* (1722), the heroine gets pregnant, but her wise woman-cum-midwife helps her to "manage" the confinement and the newborn so that Moll can marry.

Witches, midwives and prostitutes were grouped together as holders of the secrets of the erotic world—and of women's reproductive systems. These roles might be summed up in the Aztec mother of the gods and Moon deity Tlazolteotl, who presides over sex, birthing and nursing, midwives and prostitutes, women who doctor and those who tell fortunes. She also presides over "filth", including lustful thoughts and sexual impropriety (she'll hear your confessions and relish eating them up to absolve you of sin). In the classical world,

"Cunning Women...took upon them three things, as Galen, and others do witness. The first was, to make the match (there be too many of that Trade now) and to joyn the husband with the wife.... The Second was, to be present at the delivery of women.... The Third thing was, to resolve or tell women whether they were pregnant with Child or not."

WILLIAM SERMON, 17TH-CENTURY PHYSICIAN

the Latin word *sagae* symbolized this link, being at the same time used for witches, pimps and fortune-tellers (it derived from the verb *sagire*, "to predict"). The match-making wise woman's powers of prediction (of who was fertile, available and in good working order) came from her intimate knowledge of women's fertility. She knew about contraceptive techniques, sexually transmitted diseases and the early signs of pregnancy; she could bring a child to term and deliver it, or talk about herbal abortificants (if found guilty of using these, she faced transportation or worse). Wise women gave women a measure of control over their reproductive lives, and were respected for this: being a registered midwife actually decreased the chances that a woman would be accused as a witch in the early modern era.

previous page: *Ensnared by a Procuress from the Harlot's Progress*, William Hogarth, 1732, British

This engraving from the series *A Harlot's Progress* shows young women being traduced by an older procuress whose occupation in hinted at—the goose in her basket might be a indication of her trade.

The Procuress Witch

It came to pass, that one day he travelled through a dense forest, and when he came to the end of it, in the plain before him stood a fine castle. An old woman was standing with a wonderfully beautiful maiden, looking out of one of the windows. The old woman, however, was a witch and said to the maiden, "There comes one out of the forest, who has a wonderful treasure in his body, we must filch it from him, my dear daughter, it is more suitable for us than for him. He has a bird's heart about him, by means of which a gold piece lies every morning under his pillow." She told her what she was to do to get it, and what part she had to play, and finally threatened her, and said with angry eyes, "And if you do not attend to what I say, it will be the worse for you." Now when the huntsman came nearer he descried the maiden, and said to himself, "I have travelled about for such a long time, I will take a rest for once, and enter that beautiful castle. I have certainly money enough." Nevertheless, the real reason was that he had caught sight of the pretty girl.

He entered the house, and was well received and courteously entertained. Before long he was so much in love with the young witch that he no longer thought of anything else, and only saw things as she saw them, and did what she desired. The old woman then said, "Now we must have the bird's heart, he will never miss it." She prepared a drink, and when it was ready, poured it into a cup and gave it to the maiden, who was to present it to the huntsman. She did so, saying, "Now, my dearest, drink to me." So he took the cup, and when he had swallowed the draught, he brought up the heart of the bird. The girl had to take it away secretly and swallow it herself, for the old woman would have it so. Thenceforward he found no more gold under his pillow, but it lay instead under that of the maiden, from whence the old woman fetched it away every morning; but he was so much in love and so befooled, that he thought of nothing else but of passing his time with the girl.

Then the old witch said, "We have the bird's heart, but we must also take the wishing-cloak away from him." The girl answered, "We will leave him that, he has lost his wealth." The old woman was angry and said, "Such a mantle is a wonderful thing, and is seldom to be found in this world. I must and will have it!" She gave the girl several blows, and said that if she did not obey, it should fare ill with her. So she did the old woman's bidding, placed herself at the window and looked on the distant country, as if she were very sorrowful. The huntsman asked, "Why dost thou stand there so sorrowfully?" "Ah, my beloved," was her answer, "over yonder lies the Garnet Mountain, where the precious stones grow. I long for them so much that when I think of them, I feel quite sad, but who can get them? Only the birds; they fly and can reach them, but a man never." "Hast thou nothing else to complain of?" said the huntsman. "I will soon remove that burden from thy heart." With that he drew her under his mantle, wished himself on the Garnet Mountain, and in the twinkling of an eye they were sitting on it together. Precious stones were glistening on every side so that it was a joy to see them, and together they gathered the finest and costliest of them. Now, the old woman had, through her sorceries, contrived that the eyes of the huntsman should become heavy. He said to the maiden, "We will sit down and rest awhile, I am so tired that I can no longer stand on my feet." Then they sat down, and he laid his head in her lap, and fell asleep. When he was asleep, she unfastened the mantle from his shoulders, and wrapped herself in it, picked up the garnets and stones, and wished herself back at home with them.

"DONKEY CABBAGES", ***HOUSEHOLD TALES*****, BROTHERS GRIMM, TRANS. MARGARET HUNT**

"...one [of Circe's handmaids] cast upon the chairs goodly coverlets of purple above, and spread a linen cloth thereunder. And lo, another drew up silver tables to the chairs, and thereon set for them golden baskets. And a third mixed sweet honey-hearted wine in a silver bowl, and set out cups of gold. And a fourth bare water, and kindled a great fire beneath the mighty cauldron. So the water waxed warm; but when it boiled in the bright brazen vessel, she set me in a bath and bathed me with water from out a great cauldron, pouring it over head and shoulders, when she had mixed it to a pleasant warmth, till from my limbs she took away the consuming weariness."

THE ODYSSEY**, HOMER (*c.*8TH CENTURY BCE)**

The love witch

Love magic is the forte of the classical witches of whom Homer, Ovid and Virgil wrote, and none excels better than Circe, a young enchantress whose beauty cannot be drawn in words. Petronius describes her as "more perfect than any artist's dream" with her star-bright eyes, voluptuous form and loosened hair. She presides over an island where seduction so fills the air that even the wild animals seemed drugged into submission; instead of growling at intruders, the tamed wolves and mountain lions brush their tails languidly against the legs of those who invade the isle. Circe draws Odysseus and his band of sailors towards her island like a siren. Her singing penetrates deep inside the ear, and the hum of her shuttle across the warp threads weaves them into her picture, recalling the powers of the Norse witches of fate, the Nouns. She deals with the sailors by brewing a simple potion of herbs, honey and wine that turns them into pigs. But Odysseus learns of an antidote to her transformative magic, the herb moly. So Circe invites him to her bed; he surrenders and is possessed in body and mind by her powers of love-making. Her mastery of the arts of seduction is hinted at in her name: "Circe" may be derived from the Greek word *kirkos*, which describes the wheeling or circling action of a bird of prey. So dulled is Odysseus's conscious mind by her sensual world that, though she changes his sailors back to human form with a salve that makes them more young, tall and virile than ever, he feels no urge to leave the island; he can't even recall why his boat passed by.

After a year on the enchanted isle, the hero suddenly snaps to, after some prompting from his men. Circe allows Odysseus to leave;

though she won him with her fabulous love-making, she does not need to trap him, and raises the winds that steer his ship away. Using her prophesying skills, she illuminates his future path and equips him with the skills he needs to face future challenges and fulfil his destiny. Modern Wiccans might regard Homer's telling of the tale as emblematic of the balanced relationship of the great goddess and the horned god, which all couples can aspire to. Oysseus is virile and powerful, but this does not prevent him from letting down his defences and expressing his sensuality; he has the confidence to surrender to the goddess Circe. In return, she blesses him with the gifts that make him more whole and equip him to succeed in the world. She does so without losing her authority or allure and is able to let him go when the time comes.

following page: ***Circe Pouring Poison into a Vase and Awaiting the Arrival of Ulysses*, Edward Burne-Jones, late 19th century, British**

She has equal mastery over the wild creatures at her feet and the craft on the ocean beyond her window.

Fin de siecle sorceress

From the second half of the 19th century, artists reinvented the witch, seeing her darkly dangerous sexual allure not as something to fear or despise, but as a thing of wonder and inspiration. The Pre-Raphaelite brotherhood, founded in 1848, explored the writings and paintings of the Renaissance, the classical world and folk mythology, and remade the powerful witch figures it found there as unsettling goddesses with the bodies of real, erotically charged women; some of their models were "fallen" women. They painted Mary Magdalene, Lilith and Pandora, Merlin's enchantress Vivian and Morgan le Fay, Medea, Medusa and Circe. These voluptuous, earthy temptresses with come-hither arms, are enticing for more than their worldly charms; their radiance has an almost-spiritual charge, as if attuned to transcendent forces. The witch as muse allows outsiders to explore a world of sensuality, intuition and imagination and perhaps even spiritual realization. Women throughout history have been allowed, even encouraged, to have a rich interior life and to tune in to their imagination, emotions and psychic powers. And witches, unbound by society's rules of decorum, are not afraid to look at darker emotions, such as envy, lust, hatred and anger, and to express them imaginatively. Some artists gave over their lives to painting these *femmes fatales*. Like Odysseus held in Circe's sensuous spell, William Holman Hunt spent three long years completing the witch-like hair of his defiant Lady of Shalott (the painting bridged centuries, started in 1886 but holding him spellbound until its final exhibition in 1905). The Pre-Raphaelite's "stunners" (their word), earthed by their strong, sensual bodies, but so obviously aware of the uncanny and unnerving, hold a strange charge still, reproduced on a myriad greetings cards and posters.

Sublime ugliness

The sublime offers us the pleasure of experiencing excessive and conflicting emotions: to look at something horrific and fantastical is to feel both revulsion and a sensation of being uplifted, even cleansed. This is the cathartic experience of horror films. Extreme ugliness defines the witch as much as confident sexuality, and when they merge, men can feel very afraid. The witch remains intriguing to us, even today, perhaps because she rejects conventional ideas of beauty and femininity. She has an excessiveness, whether of beauty or ugliness or of dress, which is startling and disturbing. This may be a tool of power, for if we can't bear to look at her, she may do her work unnoticed. The ugly witch doesn't mind scaring children, sporting her beard and warts proudly. Facing up to this ugliness is a form of counter-magic in itself: being brave enough to look her full in the face when your instinct is to cower gives daring children in fairy tales and trial statements the upper hand; tripping her up is even more effective.

In fairy tales, hideous features or a deformity do not always connote inner ugliness; sometimes they hint at supernatural powers. In the Brothers' Grimm story "The Three Spinning Women", the "three strange women" who come to the rescue of an idle girl who cannot spin (and has three rooms filled with flax to process) have deformities that explain their superhuman ability to tread the wheel, lick the thread and twist the flax. "When the girl was alone again, she did not know what to do, and in her distress went to the window. Then she saw three women coming towards her, the first of whom had a broad flat foot, the second had such a great underlip that it hung down over her chin, and the third had a broad thumb." The ugly witches save the day.

Reginald Scot—one of the few contemporaries of the early modern witchcraft trials with an "enlightened" take on the subject—argued that most women accused of witchcraft were simply victims of their character traits or ill looks. He felt pity for the "poore women" whose chief fault was "that they are scolds", like the title character in the 1621 play *The Witch of Edmonton*, who describes herself as "poor, deform'd, and ignorant,/And like a bow buckl'd and bent together". But Scot also recognized the power of their unconventional looks, since being "so odious" and "so feared" by all, few dared offend these "frights" nor deny them anything they ask. Affronted, he goes on, "whereby they take upon them; yea, and sometimes thinke, that they can doo such things as are beyond the abilitie of humane nature…". The witch, he explains, expects "mischances", and then seeing that things sometimes come to pass according to her wishes or curses, "confesseth that she (as a goddes) hath brought such things to passe." Her ugliness has made her a goddess.

previous page: **Detail from *Pandora*, Ernest Norman, 1899, British**

This Pre-Raphaelite sorceress has an earthy physicality, but also seems aware of an extraordinary other world.

following page: ***Mother Shipton*, Artist Unknown, 16th century, British**

Mother Shipton (nee Ursula Southeil), famous witch and prophetess of Knoves Borough, Yorkshire, holding a scroll containing her predictions.

"The baby Mother Shipton was at the time of her birth of an indifferent height, but very morose and big bon'd, her head very long, with very great goggling, but sharp and fiery Eyes, her Nose of an incredible and unproportionable length, having in it many crooks and turnings, adorned with many strange Pimples of divers colours, as Red, Blew, and mixt, which like Vapours of Brimstone gave such as lustre to her affrighted spectators in the dead time of the Night, that one of them confessed several times in my hearing, that her nurse needed no other light to assist her in the performance of her Duty: Her cheeks were of a black swarthy Complexion, much like a mixture of black and yellow jaundies; wrinckled, shrivelled, and very hollow; insomuch, that as that Ribs of her Body, so the impression of her Teeth were easily to be discerned through both sides of her Face, answering one side to the other like the notches in a Valley, excepting only two of them which stood quite out of her Mouth, in imitation of the Tushes of a wild Bore, or the Tooth of an Elephant.... The Neck so strangely distorted, that her right shoulder was forced to be a supporter to her head, it being propt up by the help of her chin.... Her Leggs very crooked and mishapen: The Toes of her feet looking towards her left side; so that it was very hard for any person (could she have stood up) to guess which road she intended to stear her course; because she never could look that way she resolved to go."

***MOTHER SHIPTON, THE YORKSHIRE SIBYL INVESTIGATED*, WILLIAM H. HARRISON**

"One sort of such as are said to bee witches, are women which be commonly old, lame, bleare-eied, pale, fowle, and full of wrinkles.... They are leane and deformed, shewing melancholie in their faces, to the horror of all that see them."

***THE DISCOVERIE OF WITCHCRAFT*, REGINALD SCOT**

left: ***Malle Babbe*, Frans Hals the Elder, 17th century, Dutch**
Ugly of face and with an owl perched on her shoulder, the artist steers us to conclude this old woman in a dark inn is a witch.

following page: **Detail from *Amaterasu Appearing from the Cave*, Yoshitoshi, 1882, Japanese**
Evil is attracted to obscenity, which sucks it in and neutralizes it so that the Sun and springtime can reign again. In this Japanese legend, the Sun goddess is lured out of hiding by the sight of the female clown's genitalia, flashed for all to delight in.

The power of private parts

Sheila-na-gig is a licentious, libidinous old hag who hunkers above the key stone in the entrance arch to churches, legs spread wide and hands holding open the folds of her vulva with a grin. Such "women of pleasure" (the definition of her name, some say) first made a show in northern Europe around the 10th century and spread herself happily southwards until the 13th century: she can most easily be caught in the act in Ireland, France and Italy. And on Starbucks cups, where a version (the mermaid with a split tail) has become increasingly cauterized over the years, but is still visible to those who know.

This bawd with a belly laugh recalls Baubo, the Athenian crone who wanted to ease the sorrow of the unconsolable Demeter, wandering the Earth in search of her abducted daughter. So Baubo "relieved her sexual organs of that outward sign which is the evidence of puberty" (as Thomas Wright put it in 1865), then gaily displayed her "apricot" to the goddess, who smiled at last. The Shinto Sun goddess Amaterasu is lured out of the cave in a similar way. She has shut herself away and the Earth is dying. The bawdy goddess of merry-making Ame-no-Uzume performs a striptease dance while drumming with her feet and singing wildy, exposing herself at the moment of climax, which entices the goddess out of seclusion and brings back life-giving Sun to the Earth.

Like extreme ugliness, women's genitalia (the two were indistinguishable in the West for centuries) were thought to have the power to undo a witch's fascination (the art of bewitching with the eyes). Both can ward off the evil eye, which may be why they appeared on places of worship, and may have morphed into the horseshoe on the door, or even sexual graffiti on walls.

Uncontrollable urges

"All witchcraft comes from carnal lust, which is in women insatiable… there are three things which are never satisfied yea a fourth thing which says not, it is enough, that is the mouth of the womb."

***MALLEUS MALEFICARUM*, JAKOB SPRENGER AND HEINRICH KRAMER**

The image of a witch as an insatiable sexual being motivated by uncontrollable and unnatural urges gained widespread acceptance towards the end of the 15th century, and was perhaps best exemplified in the notorious misanthropic treatise the *Malleus Maleficarum* (*The Hammer of Witches*), first published in 1486. Commissioned by Pope Innocent VIII, it was written by two Dominican monks and sets out the nature of contemporary witchcraft and valid forms of punishment for the crime. Though not the first to express such virulent views about sexuality and witches, the book was incredibly influential.

Thanks to the technological advances of the printing press, it went into 19 editions over two centuries, and was much quoted and translated, perhaps because of its salacious detail: six of the seven chapters concern sex. There are long descriptions of demonic orgies and copulation with animals, and details of lewd or obscene acts enjoyed in the woods, at home and even during church services. There is much focus on the devil's awe-inspiring member, and an eroticizing of the sexual violence he does with it. All presented as fact.

Sorcery and heresy were women's crimes, the book suggested,

because of the female's voracious sexual appetite, itself a natural consequence of her body and the nature of its sexual organs. Every woman had the motivation for witchcraft between her legs and within her womb. That women were "beautiful to look upon" but "contaminating to the touch, and deadly to keep" would have come as no surprise to the pope who commissioned the work. Similar views had been espoused since the early church fathers started to compile the canon: the "Testament of Reuben" (*c.*109–106 BCE), which didn't make it into the biblical texts, tells us that "Women are overcome by the spirit of fornication more than men, and in their hearts they plot against men.... For a woman cannot force a man openly, but only by a harlot's bearing she beguiles him". Under these rules, the over-sexed witch need not be thought of as a wizened and toothless old crone, but could be a comely wench in her prime—and writers and artists took the bait.

The popular appeal of the *Malleus Maleficarum* coincided with the two longest periods of witch-hunting in Europe (1480–1520 and 1580–1670), and confessions began to be heard in the courtrooms of even the most remote regions that echoed the descriptions of sexual crimes detailed in the book. Wherever they lived and whatever their native tradition, women seemed to be owning up to sexual practices taken verbatim from a witch-hunter's manual.

"...to satisfy their obscene lust, [witches] burn with ardour and become adulteresses, prostitutes and concubines to powerful men."

***MALLEUS MALEFICARUM*, JAKOB SPRENGER AND HEINRICH KRAMER**

Too pregnant to live

In 1782, when few in Europe believed in witchcraft, a servant woman in a small town in the Swiss Alps was beheaded, the last witch to be sentenced to death by a court of law. But only in 2007, 225 years later, did the full story come to light. Anna Göldi arrived in the town of Glarus in 1765, taking a position as housemaid in the home of the local Mr Big, a magistrate and up-and-coming local politician, Jakob Tschudi. She was attractive, the records tell—buxom and rosy-cheeked—and served the family well for 17 years. What a shock then, when they denounced her as a witch, saying she had bewitched the daughter of the house, making pins appear in her food. Anna confessed eventually. But modern researchers studying the horrifically detailed court records leaked by a concerned clerk, claim that Anna was tortured; her forced confession a cover-up concocted by church, state and family to protect their good name and Tschudi's income. For adulterers were barred from public office at that time and the records show not only that the girl had become pregnant with her master's child, but that she was threatening to speak out. An accusation of witchcraft saved face, an expedient way for all concerned to be rid of a tricky problem. And the townsfolk looked the other way. What was hushed up then is now widely broadcast on the internet and in a museum dedicated in her memory in the town, established to promote the rights of minorities. A cross-party group of Swiss MPs campaigned to have Anna pardoned, a symbolic act intended to highlight the plight of all victims of persecution and miscarriages of justice. But parliament, like the townspeople of old, would still rather look the other way.

Erotic possibilities

Hallowe'en has become such an opportunity for sexy dressing—playing with the looks of the dominatrix, cat woman, vamp and call girl—that in 2007 the *Washington Post* dubbed it "Sluttyween". It's an old look. In classical times, witch and prostitute may have dressed in similar fashion: the Roman poet Lucan describes the outlandish, florid modes of sorceresses as being like the yellow and green dress of prostitutes. also associated with possession and lunacy. Contemporary young women say they are drawn to the "Goth" look, which styles itself around stereotypical witch garments such as black and lace, because of its sexual charge. A 23-year-old British girl said, "I got a lot more attention from guys, both in and out of the subculture." By putting on these clothes, the shy teenager felt as if she clothed herself in some of the allure of the sexual enchantress, the experience of the wise woman, the confidence of the outspoken crone and vampishness of the man-sucking night witch. Though in our celebrity-driven, porn-infused society, it might be more in keeping with the spirit of the witch to do the truly outrageous and not feel obliged to dress sexlly. Big business is cashing in on the potent mix of associations. One of the top-selling sex toys in high-end erotica emporium is the Magic Wand, a vibrator renowned for the power of its ride and its size, which many find, like the witch herself, intimidating in its sexual confidence. In 2002 there

previous page: *Harlot Seated upon the Waters*, Tapestry, 15th century, French

This scene from the Apocalypse depicts a harlot with the mermaid's signature comb and mirror. The tree beside the water hints at the forbidden fruit in the Garden of Eden and of mankind's fall from grace courtesy of another harlot, Eve.

was salacious tittering over the uses to which a vibrating Harry Potter broomstick toy could be put, and questions asked of Mattel, its manufacturer, by American's largest women's Christian campaigning organization, Concerned Women for America.

For modern witches, sexuality is inherently sacred. In 1974, the American Council of Witches enshrined it in one of 13 statements defining the principles of Wiccan belief, declaring, "We value sex as pleasure, as the symbol and embodiment of life, and as one of the sources of energies used in magickal practice and religious worship." Wiccan groups may adopt practices from other faith and esoteric traditions, such as the practice of Tantra, to explore this "Great Rite", and help to reclaim women's sexuality from the realm of the demotic, pornographic and slutty.

right: *Two Witches*, Margaret Brundage, 1947, American

Within every vamp lies an inner hag suggests Margaret Brundage's painting. Her erotic images of women adorned numerous covers of the American pulp-fiction magazine *Weird Tales* in the 1930s, and helped continue the link between witches and a slutty sensuality.

Dance of Dionysus

Interview with Lexa Roséan

Described as "spellbinding" by *USA Today*, Lexa Roséan has been voted NYC's favourite witch by the *Village Voice* and hailed by the *New York Post* as "psychic of the moment". Her first job was as a dancing snake charmer, and she was photographed in this period by Andy Warhol. Priestess, psychic, poet and playwright, Lexa has taught astrology, tarot, Wicca, spellcraft and served as oracle in her own coven. She has authored a number of successful non-fiction titles on paganism and is astrologer to *CosmoGirl* and *Seventeen* and for the magazine *Reportango*. She is an acclaimed dancer of Argentine tango, and was the first woman leader officially invited to dance in the Mundial Competition in Buenos Aires.

How did you come to marry Wicca with the dance?

Wicca lead me to the dance. I was going through a dark period and in search of direction and light I did a ritual to the god Changó—god of the drum and the heartbeat and one of the Orishas (African gods). I stumbled into Argentine Tango. A year later, one of my teachers told me that though the dance is modern, dating from the late 1800s, it had connections with an African slave dance and may have derived from the word *chango*; that's a pretty direct link! Changó and tango helped me to rediscover the passion in life.

Is dancing a form of spell-making?

Absolutely; dance is a form of love and fertility magic; look at how we dance around the Maypole and the Beltane fires and jump the broomstick. I always loved ritual trance work in covens, making up movement in the moment—running, shouting, playing drums—to work up energy. Dance is also a way of exploring our feminine and masculine qualities. We have both within us: as women, we can choose to draw down the spirit of the Goddess or the God. When invoked, sometimes this divine spirit speaks and sometimes it dances. I learned the women's part in tango, but I dance almost exclusively the man's role. I dance as leader even in Buenos Aires; indeed, I have been welcomed in this role by Argentine men. We shouldn't let gender or sexual preference limit our spiritual expression.

People think that the feet dance, but to me it's the heart. The drum beat we dance to is nothing other than the beat of the heart. Dance is a coupling, but because each connection of the heart is different, so is each embrace. There is the dance of the heart with one's lover, brother, or mother, or friend or child. Feeling from the heart makes dance a very healing form. In our community, there was a woman dying of cancer, and she danced two years longer than she should have. When she got up and dressed beautifully to come to tango and danced, it was healing for everyone in the room. For me, part of the magic of the dance comes also from the words we dance to. Much of my writing has been inspired by reading tango lyrics, *las lettras*—a form of secret poetry that reminds me of ancient hymns. Each tune evokes a distinct feeling that inspires my dancing. Tango is also a completely improvized dance. You weave your spell in the moment. Just as the witch learns her herbs and roots and then mixes magic in her cauldron, you learn the alphabet of movements and then write poetry with your body.

What about more erotic forms of dance?

In the dances of the Goddess you make an erotic connection; it becomes a sacred act, and even in times of great censorship there has always been erotic dancing. Veiled dancing fascinates me; in our time, the veil is seen as something that covers women and takes away their power, but in dance by hiding and revealing the female body, the veil accentuates a woman's power. It's extremely erotic and seductive. It's a beautiful thing when a woman feels free to express herself through the dance. The Goddess instructs Her priestesses to dance naked in their rites as a sign that they are truly free!

Do you bring your divination skills to the dance?

Once a month I sit at dance parties and tell fortunes! People expect it of me now, even in Buenos Aires. But then there have always been fortune-tellers at tango parties in Argentina: old woman sitting at the back of the room reading the tarot cards. I work both with the cards and astrology; I like to think of them as my right and left hands, and, for me, the World card is the card of the dance.

following page: ***Foxflies*, Nanakawa Sadahiro, 1840, Japanese**

A handsome young samurai meeting a magic fox by moonlight. He may wish to possess her as a concubine, but for a man and a fox to knowingly consort is a deadly sin.

The foxy lady

In Japan, the *kitsune* or shape-shifting fox, is a supernatural vixen in every sense of the word, who can bewitch, mislead or sexually possess even the most upstanding and valiant of men, including the great Samurai warrior. Or—for they do like to toy with men—they may choose to bestow on them great riches. Japanese folk tales have explored the mischievous and often lewd deeds of these outsider spirits since the 7th-century, when they started to arrive via China and India and took their place as messengers to and from Inari, the deity of the rice plant in the Shinto religion—pairs of white foxes guard the entrance to her shrines.

Fox spirits are linked to the souls of dead women, who, consumed with jealousy, anger and spite, are condemned to manipulate, tease and taunt the living with sorcery until released from their agony by the prayers of a kind-hearted person. The manipulation of these *femmes fatales* might include leading men astray by means of fox flares, supernatural lights or by possession—*kitsune-gami*—slowly waving their tails in the air until men are hypnotized into serving them or servicing their insatiable sexual cravings. Some of the vixens disguise themselves as princesses, others as nuns, but you can always tell the *kitsune* from her alluring gait and a certain "foxy" look about the eyes—even today attractive women might be referred to in Japan as *kitsune-gao-bijin*, "fox-faced beauties", a tell-tale red tail glimpsed beneath the hem of a kimono. Once the poor man realizes the nature of his situation and see his "fox wife" for what she really is, the lady in an instant turns vixen and flees. Her dumbstruck victim is left exhausted and sometimes slow of mind—sucked dry of his life-force—in a marital palace that was no more than a reeking fox's den.

笹原隼人
嵐璃寛
五蝶亭

"There was once a man who wished to have a wife unlike all other wives, and so he caught a little fox, a vixen and took it home to his tent.

One day when he had been out hunting, he was surprised to find on his return that his little fox-wife had become a real woman. She had a lovely top-knot, made of that which had been her tail. And she had taken off the furry skin. And when he saw her thus, he thought her very beautiful indeed.

Now she began to talk about journeyings, and how greatly she desired to see other people. And so they went off, and came to a place and settled down there.

One of the men there had taken a little hare to wife. And now these two men thought it would be a pleasant thing to change wives. And so they did.

But the man who had borrowed the little vixen wife began to feel scorn of her after he had lived with her a little while. She had a foxy smell, and did not taste nice.

But when the little vixen noticed this she was very angry, for it was her great desire to be well-thought-of by the men. So she knocked out the lamp with her tail, dashed out of the house and fled away far up into the hills."

"*THE MAN WHO TOOK A VIXEN TO WIFE*", *ESKIMO FOLK-TALES*,

COLLECTED KNUD RASMUSSEN, TRANS. W. WORSTER

Serpent woman

"*You* are the devil's gateway.... *You* destroyed so easily God's image, man. On account of *your* desert—that is, death—even the Son of God had to die."

***ON THE APPAREL OF WOMEN*, TERTULLIAN (3RD CENTURY CE)**

Woman is the gate of the devil, announced Tertullian, bishop of Carthage in the 3rd century. He was referring to the idea common for millennia in the church that the first woman, Eve, succumbed to the wicked serpent's wiles, then tempted Adam to sin, causing the fall of mankind from eternal bliss. Why did the serpent tempt Eve before Adam? Her femaleness made her the weaker of the two, thus easiest to tempt. She's weak because of her looks and the vanity that always follows beauty, her curiosity and gullibility, her inability to reason (she's all animal body to Adam's reasoning soul), and above all for her physical weakness. This is not only her lack of physical strength, but the sensuality of her female body (the phallic snake and unsealed, sexually active woman are a perfect fit). Eve can't help flaunting taboos: she's imperfect because formed from a bent rib, and since imperfect, always deceptive—naturally attuned to do malice.

By beguiling the first man (the image of God) with her body, Eve does the devil's work for him. And sets in motion consequences that pass down the generations, connecting for posterity the notions of

women's sexuality and man's downfall. Some early non-canonical texts have Eve made not from Adam, but from the same substance as Satan and in early Christian art a snake is often represented with a woman's head. But Eve, the witch prototype is not the Eve we read of in the Bible. In the opening verses of Genesis, Adam and his wife are made equal: "So God created man in his own image, in the image of God created he him; male and female created he them." The couple are urged by God to "become one flesh". Adam is with Eve when she eats, does not stop her, and needs no persuasion to join in: "she took of the fruit thereof, and did eat, and gave also unto her husband with her; and he did eat." Commentators since the Enlightenment have chosen to interpret Eve's "sin" as a positive act, one that sets mankind apart from the animal kingdom and makes us fully human. After this awakening from innocence, we are fully aware—of evil as well as good—and thus can make ethical choices and live independently.
In the Christian tradition, Eve's "sin" also allows for the coming of Christ, the second Adam, and his mother Mary, a figure of redemption connected with the Mother Goddess and the multitude of witch figures that resemble her.

previous page: *Eve*, Lucien Levy-Dhurmer, early 20th century, French

Eve, who has the red wanton locks of a temptress, selects an apple and is beguiled by the serpent.

"She was a gordian shape of dazzling hue,
Vermilion-spotted, golden, green and blue;
Striped like a zebra, freckled like a pard,
Eyed like a peacock, and all crimson barr'd;
And full of silver moons, that, as she breathed,
Dissolv'd, or brighter shone, or interwreathed
Their lustres with the gloomier tapestries —
So rainbow-sided, touch'd with miseries,
She seem'd, at once, some penanced lady elf,
Some demon's mistress, or the demon's self.
Upon her crest she wore a wannish fire
Sprinkled with stars, like Ariadne's tiar:
Her head was serpent, but ah, bitter-sweet!
She had a woman's mouth with all its pearls complete:
And for her eyes: what could such eyes do there
But weep, and weep, that they were born so fair?
As Prosperpine still weeps for her Sicilian air.
Her throat was serpent, but the words she spake
Came, as through bubbling honey, for Love's sake."

DESCRIPTION OF THE WITCH LAMIA IMPRISONED IN A SERPENT'S BODY,
FROM *LAMIA*, JOHN KEATS

Temped by an apple

"Thereupon she went into a quite secret, lonely room, where no one ever came, and there she made a very poisonous apple. Outside it looked pretty, white with a red cheek, so that everyone who saw it longed for it; but whoever ate a piece of it must surely die."

"LITTLE SNOW WHITE" IN *HOUSEHOLD TALES*, BROTHERS GRIMM, TRANS. MARGARET HUNT

The Latin word *malus* refers to both apple and evil. Apples and witches go together, not just because Hallowe'en and the apple season coincide in the Northern Hemisphere (hence the popularity of apple-bobbing games), but because the fruit of Eve's original sin was thought to be an apple, though not named as such in the Bible. The fruit's connection with women is older than the Bible. It is entwined with the symbolism of breasts and if you cut an apple through its belly, you find a pentagram at its core. This five-pointed star is a symbol of witches and also the shape a woman's body makes with limbs spread (men have an extra spoke that makes a Star of David). Cut the apple the other way and it reveals a core (the fruit is sacred to the goddess Kore) shaped like the vulva.

The apple was a symbol of the Greek goddess of love, Aphrodite and her Roman counterpart Venus, and represented sexual knowledge, so it's no wonder that the apple's rind and pips are used in love divination rituals at Hallowe'en and on other supernatural nights of the year. Its parings might spell out a lover's initial or the pips pop on the fire to indicate flaming passion. The red apple is especially appropriate in spells for fertility and beauty, its colour akin to the spell-binding power of menstrual blood.

In Celtic mythology, the apple is connected with the underworld, immortality and fore-telling (it is used to select future kings). With death and rebirth come the opportunity to make yourself afresh, which is the essence of the urge to divine. In Christian tradition, the apple is also a symbol of Christ, a means of redemption and the path to resurrection and eternal life. In the Scandinavian saga the *Edda*, the Norse goddess Idun governed a mystical apple land whose fruit ensured immortality.

Apples crop up remarkably often in witness statements at the trials of early modern witches. Children who accept food from someone other than their mother—often apples—seem to fall ill and even die, long before we knew the story of Snow White's witch-stepmother with her poisoned apple. It was well known that a morsel of food could open a conduit through which a witch could drain a child's life-force. Even now, we teach our young folk of the dangers of taking food or drink from strangers, whether sweets or drinks doctored with date-rape drugs. The apple is the bringer of awakening from innocence into sexual awareness. Some retellings of Hansel and Gretel seem to have the stranger-danger message in mind when they describe the witch's transformation from kind old lady with sweets to adult who wishes to harm a child for pleasure. Other retellings might regard an apple as a healthier choice for the children than the witch's gingerbread. The demons that haunt modern parents and teachers are the spectres of obesity and early-onset diabetes and their imps are sugar-coated apples.

"The apple was so cunningly made that only the red cheek was poisoned. Snow White longed for the fine apple, and when she saw that the woman ate part of it she could resist no longer, and stretched out her hand and took the poisonous half. But hardly had she a bit of it in her mouth than she fell down dead."

"LITTLE SNOW WHITE", IN *HOUSEHOLD TALES*, BROTHERS GRIMM, TRANS. MARGARET HUNT

left: ***Snow White*, Walter Crane, 1880, British**

Walter Crane's vision of the temptation of the virginal Snow White engraved in 1880 for an edition of *Household Stories from Grimm*. The witch has disguised herself to resemble a country-woman.

Barenaked ladies

"...as the sign that ye are truly free, ye shall be naked in your rites..."

***ARCADIA*, CHARLES GODFREY LELAND**

Before we thought that witches dressed in black with pointy hats, they were most commonly depicted naked. Though few accused witches confessed to it at their trials, imagery from 16th-century Northern Europe was awash with naked young curvaceous (or old saggy witches) riding aback monstrous beasts, preparing potions round the cauldron, or being nuzzled by demonic creatures. The German artists Albrecht Altdorfer and Hans Baldung Grien were masters of the genre. Look further afield—from Uganda to Bengal to the Navaho culture—and we find similar stories of witches flying naked by night on wild animals or meeting in circles to shake their stuff.

Modern witches are popularly known for getting naked outdoors, a state known as "skyclad". The term was invented in post-war Britain by the creator of many of the rituals and philosophy of modern forms of witchcraft, Gerald Gardner, a fervent naturist. Ritual nudity might be adopted by modern witches as a social leveller, a way of shedding the conventions and hierarchies of the everyday world—when naked, lawyer, cleaner and bus driver look much the same. It makes participants feel more connected on a symbolic level, too. Ritual nudity marks out a group serious in intent and comfortable with each other.

Being naked recalls the state of innocence experienced by Adam and Eve in the Garden of Eden before they gained the knowledge of good and evil; before they knew that they were naked and understood that it was shameful. It may help celebrants to explode the Christian myth of division between body and soul, and to understand that exploring the pleasures of the body and the senses is as valid a way to explore the spiritual life as focusing on the way of the intellect and mind.

As well as forging a very tangible connection to the world of nature, some witches believe that being naked raises the receptivity of the body's aura or energy field, which is directed in spell-making. It may also be seen as a mark of respect to nature, akin to removing one's shoes before entering a mosque or temple. Some people find that taking off all coverings helps them to touch their true self—the newborn in her birthday suit, full of potential—and to access the realm of pure spirit. Unconcealed, one is nearer Universal truths.

following page: ***If You Go Down to the Woods Tonight...*, Treetrunk Ltd, 20th century, British**

Painting of a naked witch lying on a branch in a forest at dark of night watched over by the spirit eyes of Mother Nature.

Scared men

"What can an aged mother do,
And what have ye to dread?
A curse is wind, it hath no shape
To haunt your marriage bed."

"THE THREE GRAVES", WILLIAM WORDSWORTH

It has always been believed that witches have the power to "unman" men; to relieve them of their virility either through spell-craft or their innate excessive lustfulness. King James I stated that witches had the power to weaken "the nature of some men, to make them unable for women." And as late as the 19th century, men unable to consummate their marriage believed themselves to have been spell-bound by a witch during the blessing. A key fear was that a witch could stop a man's flow of semen with her knot spells by tying up his tubes. So fearful was this thought that some of the first laws in Europe against witchcraft forbade "knotting" or "tying" (*ligatura*), and levied fines for those who used knotted cords. Even more frightful was the fear that witches would steal a man's "tool" altogether. Reginald Scot's *The Discoverie of Witchcraft* of 1584, is a remarkably sanguine work that

right: *Witch Performing Spell*, Artist unknown, 15th century, German
A woodcut of a witch performing.

nonetheless contains huge amounts of titillating witch lore, including on penis-snatching. He tells of a young man going to a witch to seek the return of his member. The poor man is told to climb a tree, where he finds in the branches a bird's nest, and there, carefully hidden within is his precious part. Scot tells of other nests containing 20 or even 30 such hidden treasures. In other tales, witches keep them in cosy, lined boxes, like they do their familiars, where they wriggle around and are fed oats and corn.

Such tales show an intense fear of feminine power; perhaps it is the same fear that makes Circe's story so powerful. This tale spotlights the vulnerability of the male body by revealing just how easy it is for a young woman single-handedly to transform in a trice a host of brave, strong, worldly wise sailors into a bunch of squealing creatures on four legs—and then to herd them into a pen. They are stripped of their masculine dignity and the essence of what makes us human, our ability to use words. Words are power; they bring things into being, and God gave only Adam the power of naming. In the early modern era, the woman who spoke out was a "shrew" or a "scold"; her cursing or swearing unmanned men"s right to mastery of the word and the world.

The wife on top

The first witch of the Christian era is not Eve, but Adam's first wife, Lilith. According to folk tradition and sacred Jewish texts, Lilith was not made, like Eve, from part of the first man, but from the same sediment of the Earth as Adam. This creature of filth is as assertive as Eve is subordinate, and claims to be of equal importance to God as Adam, since she was formed at the same time. Their tricky relationship founders on their sexual relations. Lilith wants to be on top; Adam, having none of this slur to his dominant role, flips her over, asserting his manhood. She, in turn, is having none of that and leaves, flying away to pursue a happily assertive, independent life with a bunch of demons only too happy to let her ride them. She lives that way still, say the legends, out every night haunting sons of Adam with her urge for ever more raunchy sex. She has been linked with the sexually predatory night hag who torments solitary sleeping men with erotic dreams.

In other traditions, Lilith is the wind-witch, bringer of storms and illness, and a night demon linked, like all witches, with the screech owl and other predatory creatures of the night. In some depictions she has talons and wings. Lilith's legions of demonic daughters are equally bird-like, flying by night as incubi to steal a man's semen and beget their own devilishly seductive daughters. Once they hit puberty, no girl is safe from the advances of Lilith and her offspring. A Jewish tale tells of a mother who buys a mirror for her developing daughter—a "dark-haired coquette"—and hangs it in her room. Little does she suspect that this will be her daughter's undoing, for one of Lilith's daughters lies in wait inside the mirror (it's commonly known that all mirrors lead into Lilith's cave, a den of sexual iniquity). The girl can't stop staring at herself in the mirror, and her gaze is matched by the daughter of Lilith, who is watching and waiting. When the time is right, the demoness slips out of the mirror and into the girl, gaining possession of her through her eyes. From there, she stirs the girl's desire so that she is compelled to escape onto the street to quench her longings with unknown, inappropriate men. She never can.

right: ***Lady Lilith*** **by the pre-Raphaelite painter Dante Gabriel Rossetti, 1868, British**

The voluptuous enchantress reclines in her bower-like boudoir fascinated by a mermaid's mirror and comb. So full of potency and life-force is her hair, that flowers seem to sprout from the tresses as she draws the comb through them.

Glossary

All Hallow's Eve 31 October. Alternate term for *Hallowe'en*.

amulet object worn on the person to ward off evil or bring good fortune; often made of metal.

Artemis Greek virginal goddess of the hunt and of women; associated with the moon and known as *Diana* in the Roman tradition.

athame consecrated double-edged dagger often used by pagans in ritual work, commonly to cast a circle.

Beltane 1 May; festival celebrating the beginning of the light half of the Celtic year, or summer.

Bewitched US television comedy about a witch that ran from 1964–72.

blaspheme to speak or write irreverently of God or to show disrespect of the supreme being or sacred objects. In certain epochs and societies it is regarded as a danger to the community requiring restorative justice.

Brothers Grimm Jacob and Wilhelm; early 19th-century German scholars of linguistics, folklore and medieval studies who collected fairy tales that still define European storytelling such as 'Hansel and Gretel' and 'Snow White'.

candomblé Afro-Brazilian religion that incorporates aspects of Roman Catholicism.

cauldron large cast-iron 'pot-bellied' cooking pot used over an open fire; may have three legs and a handle.

Ceridwen enchantress mother of the Welsh bard Taleisin.

charm words or formula believed to have magical powers when recited or written down in a ritual to bring about a specific end.

Circe classical Greek enchantress who mesmerizes Odysseus and turns his men into swine.

coven a gathering of witches; commonly thought of as thirteen in number.

cunning man/woman someone who makes a living from herbal healing, undoing curses and 'unwitching', finding lost objects, charming warts, performing love magic and fortune-telling; also known as a wise man/woman or pellar.

Diana see *Artemis*

divination the art of prophesying future events or enquiring into hidden truths using acquired knowledge or revealed information; may be a spiritual practice.

dominatrix woman who dominates in a relationship, specifically in BDSM sexual practices (bondage, discipline, dominance and submission, sadism and masochism).

ducking stool chair used for punishment of women (most often) by social humiliation through immersion in water or public exposure.

equinox approximately March 21 and September 23. Days of the year when the sun crosses the earth's equator, making day and night almost equal in length; may be celebrated by pagans.

familiar a spirit that often takes the form of a domestic animal; associated with early modern English witches.

fortune-teller someone who claims to see future events, whether through intuition, supernatural powers or sleight-of hand, and who makes predictions based on her knowledge, often for payment.

Freyja Norse goddess of love and fertility, also associated with magic, prophesy and the dead.

full moon three days in the lunar month when the moon is sighted from earth as a perfect sphere; important time for pagan ritual including the wiccan Esbat rite; traditionally regarded as a time when witches meet in groups; associated with the goddess as mother.

glamour higher knowledge, specifically of magic; supernatural allure.

Goddess female deity; used by many wiccan pagans to refer to the many aspects of a great goddess, or supreme feminine principle, who is the mother of all things.

Hallowe'en 31 October. The most important festival in the pagan calendar, heralding the festival of *Samhain*.

Hecate Greek goddess of the underworld, of dead souls and of witchcraft; associated with the moon.

hex a *charm* intended to do evil; from the Pennsylvania Dutch *hexe*, which derives from the German *Hexe*, witch.

Holda Germanic winter goddess associated with spinning, wild animals, childbirth and death; may also be known as Holle, Holde, Hulda or Berchta.

Imbolc 2 February. A quarter-day festival marking the start of spring in the Celtic calendar.

incantation ritual recitation of words or phrases to bring about a desired outcome.

incubus male demon believed to sexually assault sleeping women.

Isis ancient Egyptian mother goddess; considered queen of heaven and associated with magical wisdom.

karma action and its consequences; the notion in Hinduism and Buddhism that every act and thought has consequences that manifest in this life and future lives and determine one's destiny.

kitsune magical Japanese fox that can take human form, often as a seductive woman; these spirits can be tricksters.

Lammas 1 August. A quarter-day festival in the Celtic calendar celebrating the first harvest.

Lilith apocryphal first wife of Adam made his equal; in Hebrew folklore became a sexually predatory demon who preys on mortal men.

Lughnasadh 31 July. The night before the start of the harvest season in the Celtic calendar.

Mabinogion collection of medieval Welsh tales based on older lore and legend.

Medea Greek sorceress and wife of Jason; known from the Euripides' tragedy for murdering her children.

Medusa beautiful woman in Greek mythology turned by the goddess Athena into a hag with a mane of snakes; whoever looks upon her turns to stone.

new moon sighting of the first visible crescent of moon from earth after the dark period of the lunar month; marks the beginning of the Islamic, Chinese and Jewish months and important in pagan rites.

oracle spiritually enlightened being chosen to reveal divine knowledge; a revealed message.

orishas West African deities with qualities resembling Roman Catholic saints; venerated across the United States, Caribbean and Latin America.

paganism catch-all term for both modern nature-centred and ancient polytheistic religions; neopagan religions include witchcraft and *wicca*.

Sabbats the eight festivals of the modern wiccan year: *Hallowe'en* or *Samhain*, *Walpurgis Night* or *Beltane*, *Lammas* or *Lughnasadh* together with the spring and autumn *equinox* and the summer and winter *solstice*.

Salem town in Massachusetts, USA, best known for the witchcraft trials of 1692–93.

Samhain 1 November. Festival celebrating the beginning of the dark half of the Celtic year, or winter.

samurai hereditary member of the highly respected Japanese warrior class.

santeria Afro-Cuban spiritual tradition fusing Roman Catholicism and aspects of West-African Yoruban beliefs and practices.

scrying the art of divination, often through the medium of a reflective surface such as crystal, water or a looking glass.

second sight clairvoyant perception of future events or those in other locations.

seer visionary who can see beyond the physical realm and may prophesy the future.

Selene goddess of the moon in Greek mythology; associated with the Roman goddess Luna.

shaman visionary healer, diviner and spiritual leader who acts as an intermediary between mortal and supernatural or spirit worlds by attaining an altered state of consciousness.

shape-shifting magical ability to temporarily change physical form, often to an animal; a defining feature of witches in folklore.

siren supernatural creature who is part woman and part bird or fish commonly encountered around water; seduces men to their deaths with her enchanting voice.

solstice approximately June 21 and December 22. Days of the year when the sun is furthest north or south from the earth, forming the longest and shortest days; may be celebrated by pagans.

soothsayer literally one who speaks the truth; generally used as synonym for *fortune-teller*.

succubus female demon believed to sexually assault sleeping men.

threefold *goddess* refers to the triple aspect of the great goddess, as maiden, mother and crone.

Walpurgis Night 31 April. Second most important night in the pagan calendar in northern Europe, heralding the festival of *Beltane*.

waning moon days of the lunar month on which the moon appears to grow smaller; considered a time of releasing energy; associated with the goddess as crone.

waxing moon days of the lunar month on which the moon appears to grow larger; considered a time of expanding energy and growth; associated with the goddess as maiden.

wicca modern pagan religion of witchcraft; since the 1950s the Craft has evolved into diverse traditions with a range of beliefs and ritual practices followed in groups or by solitaries.

wise woman see *cunning man/woman*.

yin/yang ancient Chinese theory of opposing forces that create the universe such as male and female, sun and moon, heat and cold, light and dark; each principle contains the seed of its opposing force and is constantly changing into its opposite.

Bibliography

Drawing Down the Moon: witches, druids, goddess-worshippers, and other pagans in America today, Margot Adler, Beacon Press, Boston, 1986

A Short History of Myth, Karen Armstrong, Canongate, Edinburgh, 2005

Skin: on the cultural border between self and the world, Claudia Benthien, Columbia University Press, New York, 2002

The Uses of Enchantment: the meaning and importance of fairy tales, Bruno Bettelheim, Penguin, London, 1991

Romantic Poetry and Prose, The Oxford Anthology of English Literature, Harold Bloom and Lionel Trilling, Oxford Universty Press, London, 1973

Popular Magic: cunning-folk in English history, Owen Davies, Hambledon Continuum, London, 2003

Witchcraft, Magic and Culture 1736–1951, Owen Davies, Manchester University Press, 1999

The Turn of the Ermine: an anthology of Breton literature, Jacqueline Gibson and Gwyn Griffiths (ed. and trans.), Francis Boutle Publishers, London, 2006

Early Modern Witches: witchcraft cases in contemporary writing, Marion Gibson, Routledge Abingdon, Oxon, 2000

Witchcraft Myths in American Culture, Marion Gibson, Routledge, Abingdon, Oxon, 2007

Ecstasies: deciphering the witches' sabbath, Carlo Ginzburg, Penguin, London, 1992

Woman and Nature: the roaring inside her, Susan Griffin, The Women's Press, London, 1984

Night's Black Agents: witchcraft and magic in seventeenth-century English drama, Anthony Harris, Manchester University Press, Manchester, 1980

Witches, Druids and King Arthur, Ronald Hutton, Hambledon Continuum, London, 2003

The Devil in the Shape of a Woman: witchcraft in Colonial New England, Carol F. Karlsen, W.W. Norton & Co., 1998

Witches: exploring the iconography of the sorceress and enchantress, Lorenzo Lorenzi, Centro Di, Firenze, 2005

The Witchcraft Reader, Darren Oldridge (ed.), Routledge, London, 2002

Eve, The History of an Idea, John A. Phillips, Harper and Row, San Francisco, 1984

The Lancashire Witches: histories and stories, Robert Poole (ed.), Manchester University Press, Manchester, 2002

The Witch in History: early modern and 20th century representations, Dianne Purkiss, Routledge, London, 1996

The Female Grotesque, risk, excess and modernity, Mary Russo, Routledge, New York, 1994

The Bathhouse at Midnight: magic in Russia, W. F. Ryan, Sutton Publishing, Stroud, 1999

Embodying the Monster: encounters with the vulnerable self, Margrit Shildrick, Sage Publications, London, 2002

The Wise Wound: menstruation and everywoman, Penelope Shuttle and Peter Redgrove, Paladin, London 1986

From the Beast to the Blonde: on fairytales and their tellers, Marina Warner, Chatto and Windus, London, 1994

Malevolent Nurture: witch-hunting and maternal power in early modern England, Deborah Willis, Cornell University Press, New York, 1995

Transformations of Circe: the history of an enchantress, Judith Yarnall, University of Illinois Press, Chicago, 1994

Quotation Credit

Page 150 "Bewitched!" © 1964, 2008 CPT Holdings, Inc, courtesy Sony Pictures Television

Web resources

www.surlalunefairytales.com The best resource on the web for fairy-tale scholarship, with annotated tales, erudite contributors and fascinating message boards.

www.sacredtexts.com A 'quiet place in cyberspace devoted to religious tolerance and scholarship' where you can browse a growing archive of books on religion, mythology and folklore and the esoteric.

www.pitt.edu Online resource for European folk and fairy tales, arranged by themes, with new translations from Professor D.L. Ashliman of the University of Pittsburgh.

www.religioustolerance.org Site developed by the multi-faith group Ontario Consultants on Religious Tolerance for study of the world's major religions and ethical systems.

www.museumofwitchcraft.com Based in Boscastle, Cornwall, this is the world's largest collection of witchcraft-related items. Take a virtual guided tour and pay a donation to support their preservation work; the text accompanying the exhibits, much of it written by the museum's founder Cecil Williamson, is illuminating and inspiring.

www.salemwitchmuseum.com Salem's most visited museum has online exhibitions telling the story of the Salem trials and examining historical and contemporary perceptions of witches.

www.rootsweb.com/~nwa *Notable Women Ancestors* – Biographies and genealogical information on famous and not-so-famous women, from adventurers to pioneers. Includes stories of women accused of witchcraft, told by their descendants. Subscribe to the newsletter and add your ancestress.

www.deliberatelyconcealedgarments.org A fascinating site dedicated to the curation of clothing found hidden in buildings developed by the Textile Conservation Centre at the University of Southampton, UK.

www.lexarosean.com The website of 'New York's best-loved witch' Lexa Roséan. Browse her books on spellcraft and wicca, or book an astrological consultation or psychic tarot reading.

www.gptaylor.info The Official Website of the author of *Shadowmancer* and other literary worlds of superstition, magic and witchcraft, with a Christian message.

www.haxan.com The website of Haxan Films, creators of *The Blair Witch Project*.

Picture credits

2 Corbis/Massimo Listri; **5** Corbis/Bettmann; **7** The Kobal Collection/Disney Enterprises, Barry Wetcher; **10** Mary Evans Picture Library/Edwin Wallace; **12–13** Corbis/Philip Spruyt, Stapleton Collection; **16–17** Corbis/Bettmann; **18** Corbis/Blue Lantern Studio; **22–23** Corbis/ Christie's Images; **26–27** akg-images; **31** Corbis/Bettmann; **34** Mary Evans Picture Library; **39** Corbis/Cynthia Hart Designer; **40–41** Corbis/Lake County Museum; **44** akg-images; **47** Corbis/Asian Art & Archeology, Inc.; **52–53** Corbis/Stapleton Collection; **55** Corbis/Robbie Jack; **60–61** Getty Images/Fox Photos; **67** Getty Images/The Bridgeman Art Library, French School; **72–73** SuperStock Inc.; **76** Corbis/Alessia Pierdomenico, Reuters; **78** TopFoto/Warner Bros. Entertainment Inc. 2007; **80–81** Corbis/Blue Lantern Studio; **83** Corbis/The Gallery Collection; **84** Corbis/Mucha Trust, ADAGP, Stapleton Collection; **90–91** Superstock, Inc.; **94** Mary Evans Picture Library; **97** Corbis/Araldo de Luca; **102** Corbis/Lake County Museum; **105** Corbis/Hulton-Deutsch Collection; **106** Mary Evans Picture Library; **114** Corbis/Blue Lantern Studio; **116** Eduardo Sánchez; **122** Mary Evans Picture Library; **129** Corbis/Blue Lantern Studio; **132–133** Getty Images/The Bridgeman Art Library, Henry Fuseli; **135** Corbis/Blue Lantern Studio; **138–139** Corbis/Bettmann; **142–143** Getty Images/The Bridgeman Art Library, Edward Frederick Brewtnall; **145** Corbis/Bettmann; **151** Corbis/Bettmann; **158–159** Corbis/Baldwin H. Ward & Kathryn C. Ward; **162–163** Corbis/Bettmann; **168–169** Corbis/Bettmann; **170** Photograph courtesy Peabody Essex Museum; **175** Corbis/Barney Burstein Collection; **178–179** Corbis/Rainer Jensen, epa; **182–183** Corbis/Sergio Pitamitz; **187** Corbis/Stapleton Collection; **188** Corbis/ Blue Lantern Studio; **192** Mary Evans Picture Library; **196–197** Mary Evans Picture Library; **198–199** Corbis/Bettmann; **202** Corbis/Stapleton Collection; **205** Getty Images/The Bridgeman Art Library, Francisco Jose de Goya y Lucientes;

210 Corbis/Stapleton Collection; **214–215** Corbis/Bettmann; **218–219** Corbis/Bettmann; **221** Corbis/Stefano Bianchetti; **226** Edward Barber; **232** Corbis/Bettmann; **236–237** Corbis; **242** Corbis/Bettmann; **246–247** Corbis; **250–251** Corbis/Christie's Images; **254** Photo by www.sarahphotgirl.com © Zondrovon Publishing; **259** Corbis/Bettmann; **262** Corbis/Blue Lantern Studio; **264–265** Corbis/Bettmann; **267** Mary Evans Picture Library; **270** Corbis/Blue Lantern Studio; **277** Corbis/Blue Lantern Studio; **280** Corbis/Hulton-Deutsch Collection; **284–285** Mary Evans Picture Library; **291** Corbis/Leonard de Selva; **294–295** Corbis/Michael Nicholson; **297** Corbis/Christie's Images; **301** Corbis/Cynthia Hart Designer; **302** Corbis/Blue Lantern Studio; **305** Corbis/Bettmann; **309** Corbis/Christie's Images; **312–313** Corbis/Brooklyn Museum; **315** Corbis/Historical Picture Archive; **318** Mary Evans Picture Library/Edwin Wallace; **320** Corbis/Bettmann; **324** Corbis/Bettmann **328** Corbis/Leonard de Selva; **330** Take 3 Management; **334–335** Corbis/Blue Lantern Studio; **341** Corbis/Christie's Images; **344** Corbis/Historical Picture Archive; **348–349** Corbis/Historical Picture Archive; **356–357** Corbis/The Gallery Collection; **359** Corbis/Fine Art Photographic Library; **362** Mary Evans Picture Library; **364** Corbis/Francis G. Mayer; **367** Corbis/Asian Art & Archeology, Inc.; **370–371** Corbis/Francis G. Mayer; **375** Corbis/Forrest J. Ackerman Collection; **376** with permission of Isaac Oboka at www.iOboka.com; **381** Corbis/Asian Art & Archeology, Inc.; **384–385** Corbis/Archivo Iconografica, S.A.; **390** Mary Evans Picture Library/Tom Gillmor; **394–395** The Museum of Witchcraft/TREETRUNK Ltd.; **397** Getty Images/Time & Life Pictures; **401** SuperStock/Fine Art Photographic Library.

Every attempt has been made to contact current copyright holders for illustrative material. Any errors or omissions will be rectified in future editions or reprints.

Index

Page numbers in *italics* refer to illustrations

D

E

F

T

U

V

Acknowledgments

Many thanks to all my interviewees, but especially to Lexa, Ed, Claire, Paula, Graham and Rebecca Johnson, and to Ed Barber; special thanks to Suzanne 'Sam' Behling for guidance and for allowing me to reproduce her interview with Paula Keene from her summer 1999 newsletter *Notable Women Ancestors* (www.rootsweb.com/~nwa). Also to Vicki McIvor at Take3 Management and Victoria Wilson at the Royal Shakespeare Company. A full interview with Sîan Thomas can be found within the RSC's online educational resources at www.rsc.org.uk/macbeth. Extract from "Walpurgisnacht" by Yann Gerven (1992) from *The Turn of the Ermine*, An Anthology of Breton Literature, selected and translated by Jacqueline Gibson and Gwyn Griffiths, Francis Boutle Publishers, 2006 (www.francisboutle.co.uk).

Thanks to the 2007–08 Professional Writers at University College Falmouth for their input, especially Rosamund Derry, Christophe Philipps, Luke Richards and Thomas Sharpe for the Mother Ivey story (pages 218–19); Lizzie Bird for the account of Dolly Pentreath (page 205) and Doe Dahm for the research on goths on pages 169 and 352. Many thanks to Julia for the design and all at Spruce, especially Ljiljana for her continuing inspiration.